Chichester Harbour

An informal look at the last hundred years

Monika Smith

Published by Chichester Harbour Conservancy

2004

Published by Chichester Harbour Conservancy
Harbour Office, Itchenor, Chichester, West Sussex, PO20 7AW

British Library Cataloguing in Publication Data

A catalogue record for this book is available from the British Library

ISBN 0-9548135-0-2

Cover - the fishing trawler *Merlin* at her Dell Quay mooring - photograph by Jack Wetter, 2004

Printed and bound in Great Britain by
Selsey Press, Selsey, West Sussex, PO20 0QH

Contents

Foreword

A few years ago Chichester Harbour Conservancy and the West Sussex Record Office launched a major project to collect information about the harbour's more recent past before it is all lost and forgotten.

So much has already been discovered about its more distant past going back through many centuries, and has been well recorded by local historians. Of outstanding note in this respect is John Reger's *Chichester Harbour: A History* published in 1996 to commemorate the first twenty-five years of the Conservancy. Covering a vast sweep of history from geological and prehistoric times right down to the end of the last century, it could but only touch on more recent times.

So this project was set up to gather memories from local people who still live and work around the harbourside, as well as to collect together photographs, pictures, documents or just random scraps of information that might otherwise be lost.

Kim Leslie of the Record Office and Judi Darley of the Harbour Conservancy originally launched this project and then, with the help of a Countryside Agency grant, photo-journalist Monika Smith was commissioned to add to their work by interviewing just over fifty key personalities all around the harbour.

The particular emphasis was to be on life around the harbour today, on boat-building and sailing around its shores, as well as the day-to-day workings of the Conservancy through the eyes of members and officers that make it work. This new book is the result, so in this way it is very much about local people. But it also interweaves contributions about the present-day landscape and wildlife of the harbour by landscape historian Ruth Tittensor and naturalist Richard Williamson, together with the history of sailing in the harbour by writer and sailor Ian McIntyre and memories of the Second World War by writer and artist Julian Marshall.

Together, their writings and the superb photographs - many by Monika Smith - give an incomparable and lively view of the harbour as it is today, shown against its more immediate past during the twentieth century. Their researches should make this a valuable historical document for future generations to look back on our own times.

May the harbour and all that it represents to so many people survive in its present form for many years to come!

Martin Daws-Chew
Chairman
Chichester Harbour Conservancy

Acknowledgements

The production of this book has only been made possible through the collaborative efforts of so many kind people from around the harbour and beyond. Each has made their own very special contribution.

Above all I am indebted to Kim Leslie of the West Sussex Record Office who, having been so involved in bringing John Reger's harbour history into print, came up with the idea of gathering together and publishing information about its much more recent history and present-day times as told by the local people themselves. It was Kim who introduced me to the Harbour Conservancy. He has acted as an advisor throughout the project and been responsible for editing and guiding the book into print.

At the Conservancy, Harbour Master John Davis and AONB Manager Philip Couchman have both been most welcoming and helpful, seeing that everything has been in place for the smooth running of the project.

Likewise Judi Darley, Education Officer, and Anne de Potier, Conservation Officer, have always been most ready to share their vast knowledge of the harbour, whilst Ali Beckett, Publicity Officer, with her overall design and presentation, has worked wonders in transforming the completed text into book form.

No one can investigate the life of the harbour without needing to understand the life of boating and sailing. So Mike Baker of Hayling Island Sailing Club and Chairman of Chichester Harbour Federation came to my rescue, helping demystify matters of the nautical world. Local artist Roger Smith translated our thoughts for the book's endpapers into his most expressive and colourful map of the harbour.

My fellow contributors, Ian McIntyre, Julian Marshall, Ruth Tittensor and Richard Williamson have each shared their expertise, giving depth and a rounded perspective to the material that I collected by interviewing so many local people - all listed in the text - whose lives are so intimately bound up with the life of the harbour. Everyone has spoken with great passion of their love for this wonderful place and it has been a great privilege and joy to move amongst them all.

The photographs are from a variety of sources and all are acknowledged in the picture credits at the end of the book. We are very grateful to all copyright holders for their permission to publish.

Two very special friends, Professor Elizabeth McGrath of the Warburg Institute, University of London, and Avinash Puri, have always been in the background giving uplifting support and encouragement. To them, my husband Roy and daughter Sara who have all kept me going, a very big hug and thanks.

Monika Smith

2 Geoff Hancock, Northshore Boatyard, Itchenor

Chapter 1

Of Men and Wooden Boats

One of the barely surviving trades of the whole harbour area is that of the traditional wooden boat-builder. Monika Smith meets a few of those who are trained in this skill

In the early part of the 20th century, Itchenor, home to the Chichester Harbour Conservancy, was still a tiny village with little marine activity other than its commercial trade and a ferry service across the Reach to Bosham. Only a few wooden boats were moored in the channel then – a sight which today is rather hard to imagine.

One of the barely surviving trades of the whole harbour area is that of the traditional wooden boat-builder. A small number of men are still left who are trained in this skill, and they are in constant demand and held in the highest regard.

Individual shipwrights currently still enjoying a splendid reputation for wooden boat-building can be found working at various locations, including Haines Boatyard, Itchenor, at Dell Quay Marine, and at Dolphin Quay, Emsworth. Independent operators with their own workshops are Tim Gilmore and Nick Gates. Both these men were once apprentices at Combes Boatyard on Bosham Hoe.

TIM GILMORE operates his business at Dolphin Quay, renting the yard from owner David Still. Tim offers a full shipwright service, including the repair, restoration and maintenance of wooden and GRP (glass-reinforced plastic) craft. In the busy yard a big shed-type building functions as antique sales room and stocks traditional boat-building materials including timber, plywood, and all types of specialist varnish, paint and marine fastenings.

3 Tim Gilmore in his yard at Dolphin Quay, Emsworth

Six people are currently working with Tim at this yard. After Tim served his apprenticeship at Combes Boatyard he carried on there as a shipwright until 1996 when he found the premises at Emsworth.

Dolphin Quay Boatyard was started by DAVID STILL in 1972, mainly supplying

moorings for old wooden boats or 'boats of character'. There are approximately forty mooring spaces on the pretty, but highly developed, waterfront off Queens Street in Emsworth. David specialises in servicing motor boats and rigid inflatable rescue craft, and is leasing moorings to others also dealing with these types of craft. He trained as a rope-maker in the East End of London on the original rope walk at Marlow Ropes, and in the casting of boat fittings.

NICK GATES was charge-hand at Combes Boatyard. He remembers starting there in 1987 just after that notorious big storm - still so fresh in local memory. Nick had completed a year's training at IBTC (International Boatbuilding Training Centre) in Lowestoft. He visited Combes with a friend and was offered a job as 'office wallah'. After Drew Isaac purchased the yard in 1990, Nick was promoted to shipwright and Outside Yard Manager. This involved organising boat movements (including driving a crane) and the running of the yard in spring and autumn. Nick was sad to leave when the yard closed in June 1999. He managed to find a small workshop on the main road at Nutbourne.

4 Nick Gates became a presenter of the TV programme 'Getting Afloat'

In early 2003 Nick Gates became presenter of a lively TV programme called 'Getting Afloat'. Fifteen episodes were broadcast on the Discovery Home & Leisure programme (Sky Digital). The series was described as a documentary to accompany shipwright Nick Gates as he steps aboard a diverse range of traditional craft: from dinghies to Tall Ships, Thames barges to gun punts - some of the most beautiful boats in Europe. It invited viewers to follow the restoration of a 1950s racing Sharpie and learn some of the tricks of his trade.

5 Emsworth Shipyard about 1920

Emsworth once had a thriving trade of ship-building, which started to decline in the 20th century with the death of JD Foster, well-known fishing fleet owner - whose boats included *Echo*, said to be the largest sailing fishing boat ever built in the country. The Emsworth Shipyard eventually gave way to a housing estate by the 1980s.

Another yard where wooden boat repair and service are still undertaken is the Haines Boatyard at Itchenor. There had been infrequent wooden boat-building going on at the site since the 19th century, but it appears that a more permanent building and repair yard was not established until about 1912 by the Haines family.

The current General Manager, and one of the directors, FLINT ELGIE, briefly tells the story:

> *The present Haines Boatyard at Itchenor evolved from the harbourside business operated by the Haines family since just before the First World War. In 1983, however, George and Ken Haines, wishing to retire, placed the yard on the market. It was quickly apparent to local yachtsmen that this important harbour facility might be altered from its traditional use or even lost to the whims of a property developer. Resulting from an initiative by Itchenor Sailing Club, funds pledged from amongst club members enabled the yard to be purchased.*
>
> *A new company was formed and, whilst independent of the club, shareholding is restricted to sailing club members. Since then, the company has achieved its aim in maintaining a traditional boatyard service, but it has also enabled the enterprise to become a commercial success.*
>
> *In the following twenty years, the old boatyard buildings have been replaced and new machinery and technical skills introduced. The boatyard now enjoys an envied reputation for skilled shipwright work on traditional wooden boats, but also embraces the requirements of GRP yachts and, increasingly, racing dinghies. Mast and rigging repairs and renewals have become another important aspect of service, together with painting and varnishing to a high standard. Storage and moorings feature in the wide range of facilities available. The boatyard skills are also used to repair or rebuild a number of harbourside jetties for private owners.*

6 Haines Boatyard at Itchenor has an enviable reputation for its work on wooden boats

Haines is now owned and managed by yachtsmen dedicated to preserving the services essential to the ever-increasing leisure use of Chichester Harbour.

Third generation of the Haines family at Itchenor, KEN HAINES, born in 1918, still remembers the early days of change with the gradual arrival of pleasure boating around the picturesque little village. With his life-long friend, David Darley, he wanders down Memory Lane:

Grand-dad George had taken over as ferryman with a small rowing boat in 1880. Our family carried on the ferry service until the 1950s. The family home was called 'Ferryside' - which was acquired by West Sussex County Council and is now the Harbour Office.

In 1934, a year after his dad died of TB, the 16-year-old Ken Haines joined the family business as an apprentice, general all-rounder and office person. Returning from the war in 1946 he carried on work as before in the yard. The type of work undertaken was similar to that of David and John Darley. Mainly Sunbeams and Swallows needed scrubbing in the summer, repair and maintenance work in the winter months.

The Itchenor Sailing Club was formed in 1927, when even fishing boats were used for racing. In the 1930s the XOD class came in and twenty of the Z class were built at Emsworth.

DAVID DARLEY was born and raised in Itchenor. He was apprenticed at WC Young (later integrated into Itchenor Shipyard) for about four-and-a-half years, before joining the Royal Navy as a shipwright.

The WC Young Boatyard was only small but in the intervening years of the Second World War it suddenly became a hive of activity. The Vosper Shipyard in Portsmouth had been bombed, so its employees were transferred to Itchenor.

The young David saw many workers arriving from all over. Some commuted by train to Bosham, then by bicycle, and finally by ferry across to Itchenor. He and Ken Haines remember that wages were one shilling (5p) an hour or one shilling and nine pence (9p) for skilled tradesmen. Instrument makers were

8 John Darley (left) and his brother David working on a boat

also employed in the shipyard. First the Army and then the Royal Navy were based at what is now the sailing club. This unexpected number of over a hundred workers and personnel led to the opening of a very popular tearoom run by Rose Haines, doing a particularly brisk trade at lunch times.

The family business, HC Darley & Son (the '& Son' being David's older brother John), started in a small shed next to the Ship Inn, later moving to purpose-built premises. It was a small firm employing only two or three people at any one time, mainly taking care of repair and maintenance work. They specialised in the finishing and varnishing of the glorious wooden boats of that era. Darley & Son's high-class painting and varnishing afforded them a wonderful reputation far and wide, even with the international yacht racing fraternity (Sir Peter Scott, Uffa Fox, David Pollock and many participants in the Prince of Wales's Cup). Competitors for the Schneider Trophy made good use of the Darleys' skills. Darley & Son had enough work every year from October to Whitsun.

'The Darleys introduced the yacht chandlery to the village,' said Ken Haines, 'and it was the best move they ever made. They started with a shed and turned it into a yachtsman's paradise!'

When fibreglass became the new magic material, the Darleys carried on but closed their workshop in 1990, renting out the premises to others working on their own craft. Moorings and car parking became their speciality then, with David making a stern but fair attendant.

The men who build and service boats of any description, and the owners of the various marinas catering for the vastly expanding leisure industry around Chichester Harbour, have one thing in common. They all speak with great passion about their working lives.

> **9** The mock-Tudor buildings at Northshore Boatyard, Itchenor, were built in the 1930s to blend in with the village

Meeting them, one almost seems drawn into a conspiracy, let into the secrets of another world. There is an air of mystery about these men and their yards. So many riddles seem to lurk in the harbour's many creeks and hidden nooks and crannies. The lapping waves whisper old mariners' songs. The men's sun-burnt, rugged faces express serious respect for all things nautical, while their eyes light up enthusiastically whenever they spot a beautiful boat. And there are always tales to accompany such a boat: who built her, where she has been, who owned her, how well she did in racing.

10 Bill Kentell (left) assists with building *Liseta* in the 1950s

There are tales of the deeds of the old Men of Bosham, the roughness of the fishermen of Emsworth on their gun punts, the great talent and skill of craftsmen and dashing yachtsmen and the story of daring Dooge, the water gypsy.

They speak with passionate voices, sparkling eyes and knowing smiles when they recount collective memories. The fascinating history, the colourful tales of intrigue, the beguiling beauty of the landscape, the continuous sound of slapping halliards against masts and the picturesque water-edged villages make this a very special place.

Retired owners of yards and marinas hold the fondest of memories about their boating lives.

11 Noticeboard at Northshore showing the variety of work

Another Month Ends
All Targets Met
All Systems Working
All Customers Satisfied
All Staff Eager and Enthusiastic
All Pigs Fed and Ready to Fly

Across the water from Itchenor, up a creek off Itchenor Reach, BRYAN MOFFAT has a glorious view from his home at Smugglers Lane. Bryan can observe the coming and going of boats without having to step outside.

Recently retired from being Chairman and owner of Northshore, Bryan still feels a little pull from that distant yard. He started Dell Quay Productions in the late 1950s, running a successful production line of Dell Quay Dorys. Northshore was founded in 1971 with Northshore Mouldings in Havant. They relocated the boat-building and sales department to Itchenor in 1973.

Northshore built fleets of Fisher motor-sailers, the Southerly range, the Vancouver range, the MG range and the

Supermarine Swordfish 36. These days Northshore is the only yard in the harbour regularly building and fitting out yachts, and specialises in GRP hulls moulded at its Havant factory. The most unusual recent application for these skills is in the manufacture of domes for mosques.

The yard itself was started in the early 1930s. The builders, Stearns, put up the mock-Tudor buildings before the outbreak of the Second World War to blend in with the village. When war broke out their military use was effectively camouflaged from the air.

BILL KENTELL, now Contracts Manager at Northshore, joined the company in 1972. He had started as apprentice boat-builder in January 1950 at Itchenor Shipyard.

Production Director BRYAN MABB was at Northshore from the start, working his way up from boat-joiner to Production Manager. At the time they had about eighty staff, out of which about sixty were 'productives' (building and repairing), the rest being administrative staff and the sales team.

As with many other trades, apprenticeships at Northshore declined in the 1980s and '90s. Mass production with new materials and changes in working culture were largely responsible for the demise of many traditional industries. Before then at Northshore there would be about twenty boat-builders and each had an apprentice working with him. The old type of apprenticeship lasted seven years, then the young man continued in other yards to get more experience.

'You became a journeyman,' explains Bryan Moffat. 'After seven years attached to a master craftsman you would then leave the yard for another one, in order to get a wide range of experience. Such craft skills cannot be condensed into quick-learning courses. To turn out a well-rounded craftsman, he will have to carry on his learning process in other yards.'

12 David Bowker with a brochure from Burnes Shipyard and the silver medal from the 1956 Melbourne Olympics

Another former yard owner who witnessed the decline of the traditional industry is DAVID BOWKER, owner of Burnes Shipyard between 1947 and 1967. Since David sold up the yard near Bosham Quay it has stood empty and is now in a derelict state.

Like most others, this yard had changed hands a few times after it was first established by Alex Fowler in the early years of the 20th century and known as Mariners Shipyard. Fowler went bankrupt and the shed and equipment were bought by Colonel FS Burne. For the next eighteen years many small sailing craft and racing dinghies were built there, then the most numerous craft in use.

Bob and David Bowker bought the yard and

13 South Coast One Designs under construction at Burnes Shipyard, a painting by John Groves, RSMA

took possession in March 1947. With three or four employees they first took on repairs and maintenance work, then an enterprising new line was explored, as described by David:

After a year or two we were the first to make sailing clothing at the yacht yard. They were called 'Rockall' sailing clothing, selling to Lillywhites, Simpsons, Harrods, and so on. The garments were modelled on the original sailing smocks we bought in France, Brittany fishermen's smocks in Breton red, made from 12-ounce cotton canvas. We dyed the canvas in various colours and tailor Bob White from Chichester came and took charge of the clothing side. Then we took on Stanley Budd to make sails for us. My brother Bob took over the sailmaking business in 1950, known as 'Bowker and Budd', and left the partnership.

I sold the Mariner's shed, bought more land at the present Burne's site and began the construction of racing yachts which was to last until I sold the yard in 1967.

When GRP fibreglass was introduced, centrally-heated factories were required, thus spelling the end of a lot of the wooden boat-building in the various sheds dotted around the waterside. These sheds, by the way, were purchased second-hand in the 1950s due to current building restrictions and moved to Bosham from Lancing with other buildings added later.

The first boat built at Burnes under David's ownership was a Dragon called *Brandysnap* in 1952, which David raced successfully at Cowes. Dandy Napper, a signwriter from Chichester, put the gold lines on with gold leaf - even though the wind was blowing hard!

The 5.5 metre *Vision*, built by Burnes, won a silver medal at the 1956 Melbourne Olympics. A very proud David was also a crew member on that auspicious occasion. Orders followed from distinguished customers. The yard produced over sixty South Coast One Designs (SCODs). Many are still being raced at Cowes to this day.

Dragon class yachts were exported and, in its heyday, Burnes Shipyard employed over forty men, including apprentices. Before the big marinas were established around Chichester Harbour, boats were laid up in sheds during the winter.

At the age of forty-five, David started a new, very successful venture in Guernsey. In St Peter Port he opened a specialist bookshop and had a chart distributorship for about ten

years. Chay Blyth came to sign his books there and Dame Naomi James and other famous sailors visited the shop, including Adlard Coles.

A further lost boatyard, which once enjoyed a great reputation, was Combes Boatyard at Smugglers Lane, Bosham. One of the last yards to specialise in building wooden boats, it offered a repair and restoration service, winter storage, a sixty-ton slipway and sold timber, nuts and bolts.

14 Drew Isaac at the deserted Combes Boatyard - now closed - once enjoyed a reputation for its wooden boats

DREW ISAAC, once director and heir to the *Exchange & Mart* empire, had purchased the yard on a whim in 1990.

A boating enthusiast, Drew acquired a boat in southern Spain in 1988, and sailed her back to England to have a new deck fitted. Combes Boatyard was recommended to him. At that

time the yard had been there for almost seventy years and its owners were looking for a buyer. On hearing this, Drew made an impulse decision and took on the yard with its thirty-two staff. As the yard had not been making any money, Drew had to reduce the staff to twelve highly-skilled men, specialising in the repair and restoration of wooden boats.

In excess of a hundred boats were stored outside and in sheds. Some sixteen or eighteen were kept in mud berths, and on the other side of the creek. With noise and operational restrictions imposed on the yard by the local authorities, Drew had no choice but to close business before the approach of the new century. A housing development has now begun on the site.

15 Brian Fitzpatrick standing beneath the commemorative plaque at the site of the former Mariners Shipyard

9

One-time yard owner BRIAN FITZPATRICK recalls briefly the history of Mariners at Bosham:

In 1800 the site was known as 'Poor House Croft'. When the land was sold in 1837 it was called 'The Bosham Workhouse' and in the 1850s George Apps first operated it as a boatyard. Richard Giles Bradshaw, a Harley Street dental surgeon, purchased the site for £130 in 1899. Yacht-builder Alex Fowler bought it in 1906 for £150. Nine years later the Admiralty erected the yard sheds there.

In 1923 Alex Fowler built the 108-ft long *New Prince of Wales*, said to be the largest flat-bottomed ferry in the world, for Southend Navigation Company. In 1924 Colonel Burne bought Fowler's bankrupt yard and moved to a new site north of Bosham Quay. Pedalo Boats produced pedal-powered beach floats there. Brian Fitzpatrick then acquired the site in 1953 from Pedalo Boats for £3,350 and then Scovells Boatyard in 1955.

16 Andrew Wheeler (left) with Jonathan England at Dell Quay Marine

The Fitzpatrick family have close connections with Bosham going back four generations with property in Chidham, Hayling Island, Fishbourne and Bosham. Francis Fitzpatrick built and owned the houseboat *Ark* on the Chidham side. It was built on a lifeboat hull from the *Mauritania* which had been towed from Southampton.

17 Roddy Wilson surveys his yard at Dell Quay

Francis built up the business from a derelict site, employing up to twenty staff in the 1960s where, as well as repair and maintenance, they built many wooden yachts - up to fifteen-tons, and dinghies, including the Bosham One Design - until the introduction of GRP. They completed boats for Walter Rayner's Atlantic and Cape class ketches, C&N Nicholson 32s, Macwesters and Rival class yachts. They also made interiors for Westerly yachts and others. Francis owned and operated approximately 150 moorings in Bosham Channel since the early 1950s, acquired from private owners and other yards. In 1969 sheds and workshops were destroyed by fire. Some seventeen fire engines attended, and the fire, it was reported, could be seen for twenty miles. A river of molten lead flowed into the creek from the keels of yachts destroyed. The site was used thereafter as an open storage and repair yard, and eventually developed as residential homes in 1989.

At Dell Quay Marine (established in 1952), amongst the fibreglass builders, is a young man who has acquired the old-fashioned methods of wooden boat-building. A former apprentice at Haines, shipwright and wooden boat-builder ANDREW WHEELER seems happy to share his traditional skills with those of his colleagues at the thoroughly modern yard.

And now we meet the old lone ranger of the boating world, RODDY WILSON, whose face used to appear on BBC South Today's TV lead-in. Based at Wyche Marine, he caught the bug and built himself a boat in 1965-6.

In 1972 I started helping Mr Wyche, who had come to Dell Quay in 1968. Dinghies had been built here for many years in two small workshops. Apparently, before the war there were two green garden sheds here, one occupied by Eddie Martin and the other by Bill Beech. They were dabbling in selling paint and fittings and dealt in buying and selling boats in a rather casual manner.

When he was in his eighties, the late Dick Wyche built a 21-ft boat and in his last few years was designing and building model boats. Today, Roddy does repairs and moorings, in what he calls a glorious car-park for boats. There are about forty on the mud and on shore. In howling gales and all weather it can be tricky and exciting.

Modern yards appear to be thriving once they have embraced the new materials and manufacturing methods. With Northshore doing well at the eastern end of the harbour, other successful businesses at the western end are found on Hayling Island.

The Hayling Yacht Company is owned by three generations of the BLAKE family, Ray, John, and Richard. The family

18 Wyche Marine at Dell Quay

business was established in 1935 in a perfect sheltered location on the western edge of Chichester Harbour. It provides boat owners with winter storage, and repair and maintenance service for GRP, steel and timber craft. The skilled team offers the largest osmosis treatment in the area, spray painting and repairs, pontoons and seventy swinging moorings.

19 Pepe Boatyard at Hayling Island

Pepe Boatyard specialises in building aluminium craft from scratch. Established in 1988, Pepe now employs eleven staff, including three experienced boat-builders, two mechanics, three yard-hands and one apprentice.

Owner since the mid-1990s, TREVOR BANTING is very pleased that the yard is so busy. His unexpectedly fascinating job now includes delivering the finished boats all over the world. He had just returned from St Lucia when orders were coming in from Egypt, Sierra Leone and Nigeria.

The firm deals in new and used outboards and boats; all makes of outboard can be serviced and a seven-day mobile repair service is offered. They do propeller repairs, cater for winter storage and sell all manner of accessories in their chandlery.

Sheltering in a bay near the harbour mouth at South Hayling is Sparkes Boatyard, now employing sixty-five people and offering a vast array of services.

20 Pepe Boatyard on Hayling Island delivers finished boats all over the world

It started in 1933 as a little boatyard run by Ned Sparkes employing just two men with mooring space for about a dozen boats. During the last war the Admiralty took over, amongst other things testing and facilitating PLUTO. Designed for D-Day, PLUTO (Pipe Line Under The Ocean) was a method of pumping fuel across the Channel direct to the Normandy beach-heads. In

21 Sparkes Boatyard before the expansion began

1976 a mine-sweeper was serviced there in conjunction with AR Savage, Marine Engineers of Emsworth Shipyard.

After 1945, the yard carried on with Sidney Rule as Manager from 1951 to 1970. In 1974 it was purchased by BASIL RIZZI. A professional engineer, Basil turned the yard into a more commercially-orientated operation. With great marketing skills Basil saw and catered for a growing need and was able to expand the yard by building a marina.

During the heyday of sailing over twenty years ago, members of the famous New York Yacht Club used to sail across the Atlantic to have their yachts refurbished or serviced at yards like Sparkes during their European visits. Sparkes built Sharpies, Cadets, SCODs and repaired racing dinghies, yachts and power sail cruisers.

In 1977 Secret Agent 007, alias Roger Moore as James Bond, had a few brushes with a nuclear submarine on the sandbank just east of Sparkes, at a spot from where the now acclaimed Hayling Island Sailing Club operates. Fake palm trees were erected to give the impression of a tropical beach for the filming of *The Spy Who Loved Me*.

22 Nick and Basil Rizzi at Sparkes Boatyard on Hayling Island

With his son Nick now as Managing Director, Basil can enjoy semi-retired bliss but still keeps a weather-eye on the family business.

It is businesses like this that continue to bring considerable prosperity - and employment - all around the harbour shoreline and its immediate hinterland.

Today, the continuously growing leisure industry they represent might well be in conflict with environmental considerations. But Chichester Harbour Conservancy does its upmost to ensure that commerce can thrive in harmony with the landscapes and precious habitats for which it is responsible.

Chapter 2

Sailors' Paradise

Ian McIntyre charts the importance of Chichester Harbour in the development of leisure sailing

Picture the winter scene: a sharp breeze from the north-east ruffling the harbour waters. Two people well muffled walking their dog on the East Head sands. Out on the water, a fleet of dinghies racing down from Itchenor, the low sun highlighting their bright spinnakers.

Picture the summer scene: hundreds of picnickers on the East Head sands, children splashing through the incoming tide, fifty or so boats anchored in the deeper water or hauled up on the beach. Further out, masses of dinghies, cruisers, power boats and even a flotilla of canoeists picking their way through the buoys and markers – making an ever changing pattern of wakes on the blue waters.

This is Chichester Harbour, probably one of the busiest sailing venues in Britain at peak times – also, by some miracle, one of the least spoiled.

People enjoying a winter frostbite race or a summer sail with the family may be surprised to learn that recreational sailing could well have originated right here. Certainly, long before Cowes, the Hamble or Poole attracted sailors, there was activity in Chichester Harbour.

Quite probably the early Roman and Viking invaders took to their boats with victuals and wine for some recreational sailing on hot summer days. But the earliest reference to sailing for pleasure dates back, amazingly, to 1683. In that year, Charles II, who is said to have

> **24** The harbour is probably one of the busiest sailing venues, but also one of the least spoiled

owned some thirty boats, acquired the royal yacht *Fubbs*. Local tradition says that he kept her at Itchenor.

She was allegedly named after his mistress, the Duchess of Portsmouth, mother of the 1st Duke of Richmond, who settled his family at nearby Goodwood. The ship's name must represent one of the first nautical jokes, since 'fubbsy' means short and stout, which apparently described the Duchess's appearance. Author Allen Chandler says in his *Chichester Harbour or Reflections on Mud and Chi* that the royal yacht 'must have been a cheerful sight as she swung there at her big wooden-stocked anchor [with her] high poop with the three miniature stern lanterns, and the emblazoned Stuart coat-of-arms ...'.

Pleasure sailing on any scale started here in the second half of the 19th century. It became fashionable for local people to hire a boat from fishermen, and take it for a sail. It can't have been easy to step on board a rough old fishing boat with unfamiliar gear, and navigate safely through largely unmarked harbour waters.

Indeed, one of the earliest sailing fatalities in the harbour arose in this way. There is a reference in Havant Museum to the death of the Reverend Herbert Morse and three friends towards the end of the 1890s, drowned when their hired fishing boat capsized in a squall.

One of the first recorded regattas took place on Hayling Island in 1884 - on Monday 25th August, to be precise. It was for 'Open Sailing Boats ... not exceeding 16ft'. Fishing boats were excluded, so recreational boat-building must have been underway by then.

In fact, by 1912, according to John Scott Hughes in his book *Come and Sail*, that well-known yachting enthusiast, Lord Dunraven, estimated that yachting employed 10,000 people. Many of them were paid hands in huge schooners thrashing about in the Solent. It is said that the harbour oyster fishermen spent their summers crewing in the huge J class yachts at Cowes. Allen Chandler, again, recalls that Captain Prior of Emsworth crewed for the German Kaiser and that well-known grocer, Sir Thomas Lipton.

25 Bosham Quay from Charles Pears' *Yachting on the Sunshine Coast* (1932)

As the commercial sailing-craft era came to an end early in the 20th century, recreational boating began to develop in its place. Colonel FS Burne was one of the first to see the opportunities. His yard at Bosham flourished and built many small racing craft, including the 12-ft Nationals, the first of the Chichester 18-ft One Designs in

1938, South Coast One Designs, Dragons and X boats.

By the 1930s, rail travel had made it easy to travel from London to the sea, and the Southern Railway Company had the bright idea of publishing *Yachting on the Sunshine Coast*. This little book, beautifully illustrated by the marine artist Charles Pears, combined descriptions of the harbour's developing yachting centres like Bosham, Itchenor and Hayling Island, with details of the weekend rail service from London - fares to Emsworth: first class, 18 shillings and 6 pence (92½p); third class, 11 shillings (55p).

26 The explorer Peter Blake was proud of his Chichester Harbour connections

Standing on the foredeck at East Head on a crowded summer weekend today, it is hard to imagine that back in the 1930s the first complaints were being voiced about harbour overcrowding. Yachting author Frank Carr wrote in the 1930s - 'Bosham is a charming anchorage, alas now too crowded all the way up the creek for the casual wayfarer to be able to drop his hook'.

The explosion of interest in sailing in the 1920s and '30s was probably sparked by increasing personal mobility, plus a determination to enjoy life and leisure following the awful privations of the First World War. The Emsworth Sailing Club was founded in 1919 by two young Guards officers who whiled away grim days in the trenches by making their own plans for a better life when they got home.

Word began to spread, in books and magazines, that Chichester Harbour was the perfect sailing venue. The *Sussex County Magazine* in 1934 described 'the beautiful and still unspoiled reaches of the wide sea estuary called Chichester Harbour, which as a matter of fact has few of the features usually associated with the word "harbour". It has no docks, no piers, no dust, no dirt (unless you call its reedy mud-banks by that name).'

The harbour became a popular destination for what we might now call sailing celebrities. John Reger in *Chichester Harbour: A History* writes about Arthur Ransome, author of *Swallows and Amazons,* and his many visits to Chichester. Here he spent many happy days sailing in the harbour in the 1950s in his sloop, *Lottie Blossom*.

Frank Carr visited Bosham in 1929 in his famous Bristol pilot cutter *Cariad*. He went badly aground off West Wittering on an exceptionally high tide two days before getting married - but he still made it to the church!

The naturalist and Olympic sailor Sir Peter Scott raced 14-footers and other boats at Itchenor. Geoff Hayles, winner on handicap of the 1976 Trans-Atlantic Single-Handed Race, sailed from Emsworth. And the great Peter Blake brought *Heaths Condor*, a Bowman, to be refitted at the John King Shipyard. While at Emsworth, he met the Commodore's

daughter at Emsworth Sailing Club, married her, and divided his life between Emsworth and Auckland.

He was proud of his Chichester Harbour connections. Hugh Robinson, who wrote the history of Emsworth Sailing Club, records that Peter took with him the largest ESC burgee he could find to fly in each of the four ports of call in the 1981 Whitbread Round the World Race.

Because it has been a sailing centre for so long, Chichester Harbour can claim quite a few nautical firsts. Birdham was hailed as the country's first marina when it opened in 1937. And sailboarding originated not in the USA, but at Hayling Island in 1958.

27 An archive of photographs at Havant Museum charts the history of windsurfing

Havant Museum has an exhibit describing how a twelve-year-old boy, Peter Chilvers, began experimenting with a piece of wood, a tent flysheet, some curtain rings and an old wooden pole. From these beginnings, a completely new and exciting way to sail emerged.

And another first - a member of Langstone Sailing Club, frustrated by the difficulty of working out fair handicaps, invented the Portsmouth Yardstick system, still in use today.

Perhaps because it was the main centre in the harbour for racing keelboats in the 1930s, Itchenor Sailing Club has been producing Olympic medallists for over sixty years. It started with Sir Peter Scott, who won a bronze at Kiel in 1936, then Stewart Morris with a gold medal in his Swallow, *Swift*, in the 1948 Olympics in Torbay. Charles Currey, still living in Bosham, won a silver in 1952 in the Finn class, and these triumphs carried on to 1996 when Ian Walker and John Merricks won a silver in the 470 class at Atlanta.

28 Charles Currey (left) on the Olympic podium at Helsinki, 1952

By the 1990s, the harbour was recognised as a near-perfect training ground for world class sailors. Substantial lottery funding helped Hayling Island Sailing Club to greatly expand its facilities, and actively promote competitive sailing. It is one of six 'academies of sailing' in Britain - centres of excellence in which sailors can develop their skills.

The Royal Yachting Association, responsible for organising competitive sailing in Britain, also won substantial lottery funding and as a result was able to select, train and fund our competitors for the Sydney 2000 Olympics - years, rather than months, ahead of the event.

All Britain's medallists at Sydney had competed

and excelled at races in Chichester Harbour and Hayling Bay in the preceding years. Their names are now well known - Ben Ainslie, Ian Percy, and Shirley Robertson (single-handers); plus Ian Barker and Simon Hiscock, Mark Covell and Ian Walker, in two-man dinghies. Several of these were selected to sail for Britain in the Athens Olympics in 2004.

What makes the harbour such a good place to perfect these Olympic skills? John Derbyshire, the RYA's Racing Manager, who himself sails in the harbour, says: 'Don't forget, most of our top dinghy sailors begin on ponds. The harbour and Hayling Bay are perfect for developing boat-speed ability in tidal conditions.'

Mark Covell, silver medallist at Sydney, was brought up on the shores of the harbour and still lives here. 'It's an amazing place: ideal for learning about meteorology - how sea breezes develop, why the wind shifts, how it interacts with the shore. Wherever I've sailed in the world, I've seen some of the conditions I learned about in Chichester Harbour. And my understanding of how to work waves came from windsurfing days in the harbour.'

Sailing as both a sport and a leisure activity has grown tremendously over the past hundred years. When author Allen Chandler began sailing in the harbour in 1918 in an old 16-ft lugsailed oysterboat, he estimated that there were no more than fifty pleasure boats in the whole harbour.

By 1958, there were some 4,000 boats on the Harbour Master's books. By the end of 2003, this figure had trebled to 12,500. As well as dinghies (4,450) and sailing yachts (2,974), there are motor boats, sailboards and RIBs (rigid inflatable boats) - 305 of them - one of the more recently developed ways of having fun afloat.

What of the next century? It is safe to assume that the 1.5 million people who currently visit the harbour each year, and the thousands who sail here, don't want it to change. They like it as it is - unspoiled, undeveloped, and uniquely beautiful. The challenge for all those involved in the management of the harbour will be to find ways of meeting the ever increasing demand for leisure facilities, without spoiling one of the country's finest natural assets.

29 The harbour is the perfect place for developing speed ability in tidal conditions. Here Ian Walker and Mark Covell race in Hayling Bay

30 Apuldram Church

Chapter 3

Of Harbour Folk

Chichester Harbour is one of the few unspoiled estuaries on the south coast. Monika Smith finds out why so many appreciate living at the water's edge

Like many global communities, this area has seen changes during the last hundred years. Climate, wars, modern living and a steady increase in population have all affected this rural idyll. Inevitably, the 20th century has brought about many housing developments and roads to accommodate our hunger for mobility.

Above anything else, and due to another thoroughly modern concept - the leisure industry - this former fishing and farming community has now become a yachtsman's paradise. Its sheltered waters are ideal for racing and day sailing and the channels offer safe moorings, in particular for cruising vessels. All manner of cruising yachts, racing dinghies and keel-boats, to a few working fishing craft, frequent the scene.

The pretty villages and delightful landscape invite land-based activities like angling, bird watching, walking, wildfowling, painting and photography. Some folk have perfected the art of simply meandering through the villages sampling the delightful old pubs or traditional tearooms as a favourite pursuit.

Keeping a precarious balance between the needs of modern communities, the demands of recreation and leisure facilities whilst preserving this area of outstanding natural beauty, is no simple task, needing an efficient and effective organisation to attend to the many issues arising.

31 Mark Wardle, the National Trust's Head Warden for East Head, amongst the dunes

Since its creation in 1971 the Chichester Harbour Conservancy has acted as caretaker and guardian of this coastal stretch. Working in close partnership with local communities and environmental agencies, it is made up of fifteen members representing local authorities and the Conservancy's Advisory Committee.

The area is of national and international importance for nature conservation as a Site of Special Scientific Interest (SSSI), a Special Protection Area (SPA) and an Area of Outstanding Natural Beauty (AONB). Wintering wildfowl and waders - of which six species reach numbers of international importance - ensure this to be a site of particular significance.

There is no denying that this part of England is appealing and popular. Not surprisingly, most of the people living within its boundaries are taking their responsibilities very seriously and have great pride in their surroundings.

WEST WITTERING, at the far south-eastern end of the harbour entrance, is the place of annual pilgrimage for sun worshippers from far and wide. On bright sunny days the fragile East Head dunes and the attractive sandy beaches become inundated with day-trippers. There the non-sailing visitors practise the traditional seaside family favourites of bathing and sand-castle building, while out beneath the waves of the Solent hopeful divers search for known or fabled wrecks.

The stunning sight of thousands of people descending on the car park, spilling onto the beaches and heading for the dunes with their picnic baskets, must put fear into the conservationist's heart.

32 The people of West Wittering take great pride in their surroundings

Whilst the commercial wheels are turning to attract visitors - there are plenty of camp sites and bed and breakfast accommodation, with facilities and amenities nearby - and all are encouraged to visit East Head, damage to the grasses and the dune face has to be closely monitored. East Head and its rare sand and shingle spit habitat are owned and managed by the National Trust, having been given the site by West Sussex County Council in 1964.

33 Many thousands visit the beach at West Wittering on hot summer days

The sand dunes are a rare habitat in West Sussex and, because of their fragility, the most sensitive parts have been fenced off. It is an important habitat for birds. There is, however, a

boardwalk for the enjoyment of the dunes and the plants and wildlife they support.

A red flag flies at all times of the year. Because of extremely strong currents, swimming is not advised.

This area is also a popular anchorage for yachtsmen and an attractive place for walking. Most of this land was once submerged. Local tradition tells of iron rings that were once embedded in the walls of the lovely church of St Peter and St

Paul so that fishermen could moor their boats there in days gone by. A handful of fishermen's cottages give the area a timeless feel, but along the main road new housing projects have been encroaching all through the 20th century.

The Wittering Chamber of Commerce guide informs its readers:

> *During the mid-1800s local farmers tried to alter the environment and landscape, but natural elements, the tide and the wind, were stronger. Even today the sea is still changing the shape of the harbour. The bird population is vast and protected. Many species migrate in and out, stop over for feeding en route and over-winter on the salt-marsh and mudflats.*

> *The undeveloped beauty of the harbour can be appreciated from afloat or ashore, and examples of protected wildlife, environmental management and history as old as England...*

As far back as 1936 the 'Rambling Reporter' of the *Southern Weekly News* waxed lyrically about ITCHENOR:

> *Itchenor, famous land of pleasure yachts and sailing ships, has become a household word for the yachtsman and is today a veritable home for their luxurious craft. Itchenor is pleasing for those who love a combination of sea and country.*

> *There were close to 200 vessels of all shapes and sizes when I arrived. Most of them were anchored for the following weekend; others had come in on hearing that the King was staying at Chichester.*

> *High water, with all the creeks and promontories of the harbour well defined, the tall masts and overhead the distant line of the Downs, was a sight that would have cheered the heart of the artist.*

34 The Ship Inn, Itchenor, is the only pub in this popular sailing village

In the new millennium the little village is still as pretty as a picture postcard. It is home to the Chichester Harbour Conservancy, whose office in 'Ferryside' was the former home of George Haines. He was a well-known ferryman and harbour master, pilot and collector of tolls until the Chichester Corporation took over the running of the harbour in the 1930s. Just before the outbreak of the Second World War the Haines family was in charge of 130 moorings and the fame of the village as one of the most important sailing centres in the country had even spread abroad. So different from George Haines' childhood when he remembered seeing 'just a few coal boats' in the harbour!

Itchenor's popularity as a major sailing village in the harbour remains, and also forms a good starting point for interesting walks. Its large Hard allows the launching of vessels at all states of the tide. A public jetty and moorings are available for short-term visitors and a ferry service to Smugglers Hard at Bosham runs from spring to autumn.

The ferry had been re-instated in 1976 by the Chichester Harbour Conservancy, after the Haines family discontinued the service in 1964. For a while the car was the only way to to travel between Itchenor and Bosham. But the novelty of using the motor car has worn off with escalating traffic jams and a rather lengthy journey compared with the few minutes it takes by ferry. It is a popular and quick way for walkers to get across the Itchenor Channel. It also acts as a water taxi for sailors to get to and from their moored boats.

The Ship Inn now provides the only food and accommodation for visitors, whereas in olden days Itchenor had a succession of odd, homely little shops selling basic essentials from food to clothing. The pretty church of St Nicholas, patron saint of children and seafarers, dates from the 13th century.

The majority of today's inhabitants of Itchenor are in the village for the sailing and many yachtsmen have made Itchenor their weekend residence. Midweek and during the winter the village is quiet, the only activities seem to take place around the boatyards, the Harbour Office and the pub. However, at weekends and during the summer holidays, the single main street comes alive with visiting sailors and tourists.

Children's author and artist ROGER SMITH, who has lived here for many years, recently helped compile a history of the population for the *Village Design Statement*, published in 2004, and interviewed about twenty-five locals around the village. He says that today's population of retired professionals gives it all a strangely 'suburban' feel. Most are skilled 'movers and shakers', and their protest power can be influential in preventing undesirable new developments.

35 Roger Smith **36** Barbara Payne (left) and Ivy Noyce **37** the Stearn family (left to right) Alan, Roger, Peter and Richard

One of Roger's subjects was ninety-year-old Barbara Payne, who has lived in Itchenor since 1928. Her family originates from Surrey: 'Father was a keen sailor and purchased an "X" at Itchenor. During their visit here mother saw beautiful marigolds in a window, fell in love with the house and purchased it on the spot. The Georgian property, "The Bollards", was hired out to shipyard workers during the war.' It is home to Barbara to this day.

Thanks to her father's passion, Barbara has had sailing in her blood from early childhood.

'Once you are on the water you become one with nature, you leave the cares of the world behind', Barbara enthuses.

She has seen five shops come and go in the village, mainly in peoples' front rooms. Since visiting sailors need supplies, the lack of a decent shop has been a problem for a long time now.

Ivy Noyce (86) grew up in Itchenor and vividly remembers childhood in the pleasant, quiet street. She said much change has taken place, more than anything she feels the sheer volume of people and traffic has greatly increased. Her husband, George, was one of the local men working in the shipyard during the war.

ALAN STEARN is another one of a few original villagers left. Alan's father, Albert (Bert), built Itchenor Shipyard for the then site owner, Mr Grasbye (inventor of the Venner Timeswitch). He asked Bert for a plan, a price and then for the building to start all in a space of a long weekend in 1936. Rumour has it he knew a war was coming, as he asked for the commercial buildings to blend in with the village. During the Second World War all local skilled carpenters and joiners and local lads with a trade were hired by the Admiralty, who took over the yard to build motor launches.

In the 1920s, Bert rented the rambling old property, 'Redlands', where Alan was born. Its huge hall was chilly all the time as there was no heating other than the big fireplace. Bert married the Ship Inn publican's daughter, they had three children, Alan and two girls. Alan remembers herding his grand-dad's cows on Shipton Green. As a young man he joined his dad in the business and took over from him in 1962. Alan was a Lance Corporal in the Home Guard during the Second World War, his dad Bert a Warden and Fireman.

Alan remembers that, in the 1940s and '50s, he spotted Hollywood movie stars in fancy cars driving past his carefully tended lawn. Relatives of actor Gordon Harker lived further down the village and Alan once spotted the legendary Stewart Granger and his entourage stopping at the green to ask for directions.

38 Birdham Pool is said to be the oldest marina in the country

Until the 1960s the Stearns built many houses around the village. In 1972 Selective Employment Tax encouraged many of the labourers to go self-employed and Alan phased out the building business and started a yard for the trade. The business is still flourishing today with two of Alan's sons, Richard and Roger, in charge and grandson Peter learning the trade.

BIRDHAM is not so much a village as two marinas surrounded by a few older dwellings and some 20th-century housing estates. Birdham Pool was built in the 1930s when an

18th-century tide mill ceased work and its mill pool became the yacht basin.

It is said to be the oldest marina in the country. A short distance away, via a lock-gate over the disused Chichester Canal, Chichester Marina lays claim to be the second largest marina in the UK. Gone are the signs of former activity as the site of important shipbuilding for Nelson's Navy, where a nearby oak forest once supplied ready material.

The marina, known as Chichester Yacht Basin, is home to many splendid vessels and plenty of thriving marine-related businesses. Oceans of masts are a stunning sight to behold. Chichester Yacht Club holds all-year-round events

39 Locking-out at Chichester Marir

for dinghy, motor and yacht sections, including the Snowflake dinghy racing series in winter. At the eastern end of the marina is an area of marshy grassland, home to many wetland birds, including waders.

From about 1823 the Chichester Canal was well used by local merchants, but the coming of the railway in 1846 soon made the canal redundant. These days intriguing houseboats sit on its still waters and herons frequent its silty banks.

A beautiful canal-side towpath takes walkers into Chichester, along a spot famously captured by the artist Turner during his stay at Petworth House in the late 1820s. Narrowboat trips, rowboating, canoeing and angling have replaced the spectacle of 150-ton coal vessels once so prolific on this four-mile stretch of water.

In the distant past DELL QUAY played a large role as a major landing place for the port of Chichester, whereas today it's a sleepy backwater mostly known to yachtsmen, and only discovered accidentally by the odd straying tourist. The 17th-century Crown & Anchor still has a timeless quality about it, even the original and very popular game of 'ringing the bull' is still in the bar. The Dell Quay Sailing Club was formed after a gale in 1925 wreaked havoc with moored boats. Today it is flourishing more than ever. Since 1999 the Harbour Conservancy Education Centre has been based on the quay in a converted storeroom and is a wonderful all-weather study centre with glorious views.

40 The 17th-century Crown & Anchor Inn at Dell Quay has a timeless quality about it

APULDRAM sits snugly north-east up the creek. The marshland east of Chichester Marina is a nesting site and haven for a variety of birds and other wildlife. The Friends of Chichester Harbour built a hide overlooking the marsh in 1997 as a memorial to their former Chairman, Peter Catlett, naturalist and environmentalist.

The Sawday family have been tenants of church-owned Apuldram Manor Farm for two generations. Matt Sawday

(40), was the youngest of five children born and raised at the beautiful Jacobean house (believed to have been built by a Dutch trader) and now his own three children share the same privilege. The farm covers 650 acres, mostly arable and dairy with approximately 150 cows (supplying Marks & Spencer with GM-free milk). Matt's father, Ted, used to employ five staff and grew mainly cereals. Thirty years ago harvest time played a big part in the farmer's calendar, but things have changed since. Now Matt has three staff and grows mainly potatoes and lettuce. His wife, Lorraine, has recently started a holiday lets business, 'Quay Quarters', in the converted farm buildings where Matt's mother, Diane, once developed a rose nursery. Matt's brother, Jonathan, now looks after the special Apuldram Roses, grown in the old apple orchard, with a mail-order business.

41 The Sawday Family have been tenants of Apuldram Manor Farm for two generations

Matt works closely with Chichester Harbour Conservancy on a stewardship agreement. Reed beds, walk access, a small pond, waterside grazing on the marshland and a dew pond on his land all form another part of the Area of Outstanding Natural Beauty. The picturesque parish church of St Mary the Virgin was restored in 1999.

Where once coastal craft carried corn to the mills at FISHBOURNE, this village at the furthest end of the creek has entered the history books for a recent and significant discovery. From a major archaeological dig in the 1960s, the well-preserved remains of a Roman Palace were revealed. It is claimed to be Roman Britain's largest domestic building,

42 The Fishbourne bike shop adds to the relaxed feel of the village

sumptuous home to King Tiberius Claudius Togidubnus in about 75 AD. It holds the largest collection of in-situ mosaics in Britain and attracts world-wide attention.

Today's relaxed Fishbourne village sits largely along the main road, having slowly developed since around 1700. A tranquil millpond is the only reminder of a once dominant water-based past. A pub-

restaurant, a contemporary art gallery and a popular bicycle shop give it a distinctly modern feel without sacrificing its old-world looks.

The water-fronted part of romantic BOSHAM is the landlubber's favourite. The fact that its sea-fronted road gets flooded every high tide is a great source of amusement for visitors and locals alike. It is often jokingly referred to as 'the Bosham car-wash'! This village is quite likely the most photographed and painted place in the entire harbour. Justifiably, the inhabitants guard this pretty village closely.

Its history is as colourful as its present-day appeal. The much-admired church of the Holy Trinity is claimed to be one of the oldest Christian sites in Sussex and features in the Bayeux Tapestry. Legend has it that King Canute had his famous experience with the tides right here at Bosham. An intriguing 20th-century puzzle presents itself with the war memorial. Normally far more men are listed for the First, rather than the Second, World War, but in Bosham the reverse is the case. Local resident and former Chairman of the Friends of Chichester Harbour, Bill Woodburn, suspects that this might be due to the large increase in population between the two wars.

43 David West, Bosham's Water Bailiff, out walking the village's water courses, with his dog Frieda and fellow resident Bill Woodburn. Following recent flooding, David was appointed by the Parish Council to keep a regular eye on local water levels

Bill also points out a few other interesting spots. On the meadow in front of the church used to be Apps Shipyard, where oyster smacks were built in the late-19th century. Remains of the slip can still be seen today. Remains also of oyster beds are visible from the air at low tide, as silent witness to a once prolific and prosperous trade. The local oyster trade was second only to Whitstable until its decline in 1922 due to an attack of limpets.

Some Bosham men worked on the trading ketches, either locally or joining trips to the West Country's tin mines. During the summer most fishermen crewed on big yachts owned by the gentry and often named their humble homes after such yachts. Cruisers and racing dinghies beautify the scene around the 18th-century wharf to this day.

44 Bosham looks towards the sea, Chidham towards the land - a local saying

Former yards like Mariners had to give way to new dwellings. The village grew in the 1930s and then again in the '60s and '70s. When new housing developments in old fields took place in 1964, the AONB (Area of

Outstanding Natural Beauty) was put in place and managed to halt indiscriminate building with a 'settlement policy' and preservation orders.

Of all local historians and authors, Angela Bromley-Martin has gathered together the largest privately-held archive of material on Bosham's history. The naval widow's home overlooks the Chichester Channel and her knowledge of the area is formidable. She has written several books on the history of Bosham and about the Bosham One Design - a group of wooden yachts, all designed to the same specifications. The fact that she is working on yet another history book of Bosham only highlights the incredibly rich past of this fascinating village.

One aspect features prominently here, the Men of Bosham, as Angela explains:

45 Local historian Angela Bromley-Martin has a large archive on Bosham's history

Once the Men of Bosham had privileges long before Domesday Book was compiled. They were exempt from paying for all kinds of tax, which included freedom from paying mooring fees for their boats throughout the Kingdom. Free anchorage in Chichester Harbour is today the only privilege left for such Men, who have to be born in Bosham, the son of a Man of Bosham, and to earn their living by the sea. Naturally, only a few remain today, with Simon Combes being almost the last one.

Still mainly used as fertile farmland, CHIDHAM takes great pride in its rich fields and meadows. The village lies on a loop-road, half way down the peninsula across Bosham Channel. The church dates from the 13th century and nearby stands the large 17th-century Manor House. Around the corner at the Old House At Home - an inn of some local standing - the landlord brews his own Chidham beer.

46 Diana Beale still lives in the family home at Cobnor, taking an active interest in local affairs

The late Martin Beale, Cobnor landowner, gave a considerable slice of land on the southern tip for the development of sailing facilities. He wanted to raise awareness of the delightful harbour and for all to be able to enjoy it. Here at Cobnor, Martin used to run a sailing school with over 200 dinghies and, during that time participated in the Olympic trials. He founded

Cobnor Activities Centre and was also chairman of the Conservancy from 1978 to 1981.

Back in the '50s the Thames barge *Pride of Sheppey* was purchased as a training ship for the Activities Centre and, next door, the Christian Youth Enterprise was originally based on an old minesweeper. A new purpose-built centre is now in place, catering for underprivileged and disabled youngsters and nurturing the appreciation of outdoor pursuits.

47 Most of Prinsted village is a conservation area

Martin's daughter, Diana, still lives with her family in the large rambling Regency home, Cobnor House. She takes great interest in local affairs and was a trustee of the Activities Centre her father established. Her parents also gave land to the community to build a thriving village hall. Diana likens her beloved home to paradise on earth: 'Sometimes from my bedroom window I can see a few deer swim across Bosham Channel - to me this is heaven and I feel very privileged to live here!'

Diana also manages four holiday cottages with special access for those with impaired mobility. On Cobnor land is a small caravan club and campsite for organised local groups like the Emsworth Cadets. Emphasis is on wheelchair accessibility, to match the Conservancy's efforts in recently installing a special wheelchair footpath by the waterfront. Diana is involved with the leisure and conservation side. Her present concerns are woodland regeneration and green and sustainable tourism. Jacob sheep graze on her fields as part of a conservation-farming project to aid local wildlife.

48 Peggy Stuart outside her church on Thorney Island

With its proximity to Portsmouth, naval personnel were attracted to settle in the select villages around Chichester Harbour. Long-standing PRINSTED resident Peggy Stuart was such a naval wife and still loves her home dearly.

Most of the centre of the village is 17th century and a conservation area, with remaining examples of fine architecture to be found in its interesting variety of houses. Peggy's home had once been part of a farm, then it was a sweet shop and later a coal merchant's. Most of the dwellings in the centre of the village were once farms. There used to be a

49 Entry to Thorney Island along the public footpath is through an MOD security gate

private school, started in 1952 and sold in 1971. There is no post office, shop or pub in Prinsted, and so for these purposes the hamlet is very much a part of Southbourne village which, being along the main road with modern shops, has a far more dominant presence.

At the southern end of Prinsted lies THORNEY ISLAND, which played a big part as a Battle of Britain base. Its villagers had been re-housed on the mainland and old cottages gave way to aircraft hangers and runways. After the war the Royal Air Force carried on using it as a training base. On moving there in 1956, Peggy remembers hearing planes doing circuits and landing with noisy bumps at least twice a week.

Another unusual role for the island occurred in the 1980s with the arrival of the Vietnamese 'Boat People'. They were accommodated in the then disused Officers' Mess, and the island school was opened for the children to be taught basic English and introduced to English customs.

However, in 1984 Thorney Island renewed its association with the Armed Services and became an Army base, Baker Barracks, with the arrival of the Royal Artillery and their families. St Nicholas church now performed the role of a garrison church with the first appointment of a resident chaplain in 1992.

In 1995 the disused Rectory was converted into a church centre for the use of Army personnel and their families, and for civilians like Peggy who live locally within the parish and who worship regularly at the church.

Both Peggy's daughters were married in Thorney's old village church - the island's last link with bygone centuries. She visits it regularly to tend the flower arrangements. In order to get there Peggy has to ask permission from the Army, and obtain the key to the church from the guardroom. On the north side of the church in the cemetery are war graves of both British and German military personnel.

For hikers and bird watchers a public footpath gives access around the island, but it is strictly limited to the shoreline path. Entry is through an MOD security gate. The seven-mile circuit of the island affords fine views of the harbour and many thousands of waders and wildfowl can be observed in these tranquil surroundings. Pilsey Island, just south of Thorney, is leased to the RSPB and access is restricted.

On the north-western end of Chichester Harbour, EMSWORTH is another attractive part which evokes a passionate reaction in local historians.

'Oysters! JD Foster! PG Wodehouse!' they exclaim and, before you know it, the tales unfold.

Once a busy port for trading coal, timber and flour, it was also famed for its oysters, closely rivalling those of Great Yarmouth as the best in the land. But when Emsworth oysters were served to the Dean of Winchester in 1902, he and a number of others died of typhoid. Sewage contamination, after an accidental discharge, was to blame.

The sale of oysters was banned until the new sewage scheme was opened in 1914, but Emsworth oysters never recovered their previously glorious reputation.

50 Emsworth's Coal Exchange pub

As effects of the industrial revolution took hold in England and seafaring commercial traffic declined, it also took its toll on the local fishing industry. Back in the early 20th century Emsworth was still a thriving fishing port. The biggest fleet owner, JD Foster, built his own innovative boats and created some of the finest fishing vessels - including the famous oyster smack *Echo*, at 110-ft said to be the largest sailing boat for fishing ever to work out of any English port.

After the oyster scandal, fishing in Emsworth declined further for the smaller fleets. But the Fosters carried on importing French oysters to London via Newhaven and, back at Emsworth, as timber merchants, alongside other industries and shipyards down King Street. Sail, rope and tent making, sawmills, a brewery, plenty of blacksmiths and a coal merchant were to be found there. Only a few remains from these times can be seen today. Modern housing developments now replace these old commercial sites. Rumours of rough and rowdy behaviour amongst the fishermen and of King Street not being a safe place to walk down, originate from the sailing gentry from Bosham-side after too much fine port! There is, however, little evidence of this today in the extensive oral history recordings at Emsworth Museum. The museum, housed since 1988 in the old fire station, tells the town's colourful history in great and fascinating detail.

Not to be forgotten is the contribution world-famous writer PG Wodehouse made to this pretty little town. PG (Sir Pelham Grenville Wodehouse, 1881-1975) lived in Record Road for

51 Emsworth Slipper Mill Pond

ten years, marked by a blue plaque. He used local place names for his 'Jeeves and Wooster' books, setting his novel *The Little Nugget* in Emsworth House School. He also bestowed the town's name on one of his most celebrated characters, Lord Emsworth.

Modern Emsworth is a very popular sailing centre with two large sailing clubs and a 230-berth marina. Artists and tourists are attracted to this pretty little town and its centre which is now a conservation area of 'Outstanding Status' - with eighty-four listed buildings and a further eighty-five ranked as noteworthy. Architectural historian Sir Nikolaus Pevsner, in his Hampshire volume of *The Building of England* series, has described the old port's 'intricate pattern of streets and alleyways leading to different parts of the waterside', with King Street 'which epitomizes Emsworth' and Tower Street 'the most delicious inland backwater' in the town.

In winter migrating birds stop off on the salt marshes around the foreshore, and Brent Geese, Shelducks and Bar-tailed Godwits can be observed. Naturalists and walkers take delight in the choice of water-fronted or landward walks available, with tidal mill ponds and Brook Meadow east of the River Ems. The harbour is well used by sailors and in early August a Dragon Boat racing festival attracts many spectators.

These days a delicate balance is struck between the still active fishing industry and conservation requirements. RIB patrol vessels cruise the fishing fleet and inspect their catch. All oysters less than 70mm in diameter are returned to the water. Chichester Harbour has very specific environmental conservation protection as part of the Solent European Marine Site.

A public jetty was opened by Chichester Harbour Conservancy off the quayside promenade in 1995. Further west is an attractive wet area of reeds and willow woodland, a perfect haven for wildlife.

The large solitary tower visible from the A27 is the only remains of WARBLINGTON CASTLE, built around 1525, and destroyed during the Civil War by the Parliamentarians in 1643. Warblington's modern face most likely appeared around 1900 when the building of new housing took place on what is now the north side of the A27.

52 The Hayling Billy line during the Big Freeze of 1963

Approaching LANGSTONE from Emsworth along the coastal path, the dominating view is that of the 18th-century Langstone Mill, now a private house. A few remains of flat-bottomed gravel barges are still visible rotting in the mud. The Little family founded a business at Langstone Quay (originally part of the port of Havant) in the 1840s and continued to bring cargoes of shingle, coal and manure to the wharf until 1939.

1824 saw the completion of a wooden toll bridge with a central swing span allowing vessels to pass, as a deeper dredged channel enabled the passage of barges to Chichester. The modern link to Hayling Island was completed in 1958, able to cope with the demands of modern traffic, but not allowing sailing craft through. The Hayling Billy railway line took passenger trains across the water from 1867 until 1963 when it was closed by Dr Beeching's cuts. A 'train ferry', an old steamer which carried coal trucks between Langstone and the Isle of Wight, was in operation between 1885 and 1888. Glorious views over the harbour can be enjoyed from the 17th-century Royal Oak public house and the Ship.

HAYLING ISLAND used to be regarded as a fashionable bathing resort, with four miles of glorious beach and pretty beach huts for hire along the seafront.

Only the island's eastern side is part of Chichester Harbour. It is the more quiet and less frequented part with Northney Marina, Hayling Yacht Company, Pepe, Wilsons and Sparkes for the yachtsmen. The very southern tip is also home to a recently rebuilt and very popular sailing club.

53 Old wooden house at Langston

In the past, Hayling was known for the medieval Great and Little Salterns which were salt pans for the conversion of seawater into salt by evaporation (disused in the late-19th century). North Hayling church, St Peter's, dates from about 1140 and is in typical Norman style. St Mary's in South Hayling dates back to the 13th century.

There is a saying on the island that 'in the 1800s a man could swim his horse across to the Witterings at slack water'. Now he must ride or drive twenty-five or so miles around the harbourside.

A well-known local personality has written a charming booklet called *Hayling, An Island of Laughter and Tears*. Noel Pycroft was born on Hayling in 1928, has lived there ever since and followed his family's occupation of brick-making from boyhood until 1989. More personal reminiscences of Hayling Island are kept in the extensive oral history archives at Emsworth Museum.

The Hayling Island RNLI Lifeboat Station works closely with the Chichester Harbour Conservancy.

Nigel Roper, after twenty-seven years' service as the Station Honorary Secretary and Launching Authority, speaks with passion and pride about the RNLI:

In the early days we had lifeboats pulled to sea by two teams of horses, which came most likely straight from work in the fields, like the men. A boy on a bike would cycle around ringing a bell and two lots of four maroons were fired to alarm the workers in the fields. Most of them were local fishermen or farm hands. They came on bikes,

or ran to the lifeboat station. The horses pulled out the boat, which weighed about eight tons. There was no engine, so they had to sail or row. In rough seas you can imagine the hard work this meant.

By 1924 two new motor lifeboats had been established at Bembridge and Selsey and so the old-fashioned Hayling boat was taken out of service. In 1975 a new lifeboat station was inaugurated as an inshore station. Modern response time is about seven to eight minutes from 'lock-up' to hitting water.

54 Graham Raines, Senior Helmsman (left) and Nigel Roper, Station Honorary Secretary, at the Lifeboat Station, Hayling Island

Recreational boating has increased rapidly since the late '60s and the average size of boats has also increased from twenty-six to thirty-five feet.

In the old days they used charts and parallel rules. Now they use GPS (Global Positioning Satellite) and many yachts have electronic charts on their screens.

Since the station was first established in 1865 the lifeboats from Hayling Island have saved over 580 lives. Today, there are three crews, each working on a three-week rota system. The men and women come from all walks of life, boat-builders, bosuns, boatyard-hands, school teachers, bus drivers, mechanics, builders, computer operators, students, farm workers and many more. Amongst our team we also have a doctor and a paramedic, all others are trained first aiders. All of them are volunteers who give their time and effort for little or no financial reward. We depend entirely on donations to keep us in service.

We house two inshore lifeboats, the Atlantic 75 class B712 Betty Battle *and the D class* Leonard Stedman, *with their tractors, launching and recovering cradles.*

The crews can face thirty-foot waves, blizzards, force nine gales and sub-zero temperatures - when they are asked to help they never hesitate.

To have such selflessly devoted individuals in a place of such great beauty laced with potential danger is of extreme importance. What seems like a tempting, alluring seascape one moment can rapidly turn into a tempest the next, and anyone - even an experienced sailor - can fall victim to unexpected circumstances.

Knowing there are skilled rescue teams nearby must fill any sailor's heart with warm comfort. Under the watchful eyes of both the RNLI and the Conservancy, the harbour remains a safe home and playground for all.

55 War graves at Thorney Island

Chapter 4

Our Harbour War

Chichester Harbour, usually regarded as a quiet backwater, sprang into life during the Second World War. Julian Marshall looks at the important role the harbour played in the war

Gulls swoop and stall, finally landing on the strip of earth turned by the tractor. Just so had those fragile planes high in the June sky zoomed, dived and fallen in the dog-fights over Sussex in 1940. Here beside the footpath is a fresh reminder of those times: a new stone, red poppies and a plaque commemorating a twenty-three-year-old Polish airman shot down into this stubble field at Stoughton. The citation reads 'He fought for Britain, Poland and for Freedom'.

All around the harbour others were engaged in the fight. At Apuldram 300 acres of field behind the Black Horse pub were requisitioned for an ALG (Advanced Landing Ground), a real misnomer for it was extremely basic! The main runway was 4,800-feet long, laid east-west. A 'Somerfield' track, it was made of steel mesh lying on the grass. Four 'Blister' hangars (like modern pig farm shelters) and tents for pilots, crews and ground staff completed the airfield. Mobile red and green lamps were used, there were no fixed landing lights. In May 1943, Typhoon fighter-bombers arrived on site, to be followed by three squadrons of Free Czech Air Force of the RAF's 84 Group, flying modified Spitfires with bomb racks. Famous for their fighting spirit, Squadrons 310, 312 and 313 specialised in destroying German armoured trains and marshalling yards. General Eisenhower visited here while staying at the Ship Hotel, Chichester, between 19th-22nd April 1944 - addressing the crews at a base which to him must have appeared incredibly Heath-Robinson!

56 Junkers 88 shot down at Bosham on 21st September 1940

Downstream at the canal, Chichester Yacht Company was taken over by the Admiralty under the Emergency Powers (Defence) Act and its equipment dispersed for use elsewhere. The present Chichester Marina, then a gravel-pit, was deliberately flooded, together with adjoining fields, to confuse Luftwaffe navigators.

At Birdham Pool, the shipyard was busy with landing-craft maintenance, the hefty turn-table spinning the finished boats down the slipway and into the water. Gone were all the pleasure boats; hauled out or laid up along the canal, any useful craft being requisitioned.

Combes Yard on Bosham Hoe had two 60-ft derricks. Here LCAs (Landing Craft Assault), the smallest of the breed, were built. LCAs had engines aft and a ramp at the bow, let down for troops to disembark quickly; 42-ft long, each carried about forty-five men. Buoyancy was packed in along the sides which was also supposed to give some protection against gunfire - this was 'onazote', a nasty brown manufactured padding, which turned out to be highly inflammable!

Across the water at Itchenor Shipyard (now Northshore) the big sheds were humming with activity behind the barbed wire fencing reaching to the waterfront. Definitely a 'hush-hush' area. Here Fairmile Type B fast motor launches were constructed, their Hall-Scott Defender engines sent from the USA. Opening up the crates was a rare treat for the workers, who found packets of cigarettes stowed amongst the wadding - bounty indeed! Itchenor had its excitements as well as its Security Zones; a Liberator which had crashed into the harbour was towed to the Hard with bodies still inside - when the demolition gang finally set to work, it was with oxyacetylene: the aluminium fuselage flared up in a brilliant white flame - an unexpected firework display. Another plane, a Halifax, huge and unwieldy out of its proper element, was also brought ashore and 'secured' to a handy telephone pole - opposite the present Harbour Office. Warnings were airily dismissed. It was all 'ticketty-boo' until the tide rose and the current tugged at the heavy plane's carcass. Down came pole and wires, putting the only telephone in the village out of action yet again.

Haines Yard was closed, their shipwrights all in the Forces, but Rose Haines at No 5, The Street, was busier than ever with socials and dances held in her tearoom; with weekly film shows put on by the RN occupants of the Sailing Club, Itchenor had never been so lively! The Army and Fire Brigade were there too, in commandeered houses: a pink cottage opposite 'Dobbies' was home to the firemen - and it was burned down! Between July 1940 and May 1944 there were sixty-seven major raids on Portsmouth, which meant plenty of 'fall-out' in adjacent areas. Showers of incendiaries (about ten-feet tall) dropped around Itchenor and Birdham - some hitting cows. A stray bomb blew up yachts in Itchenor's mud berths and showered wreckage along the sea-wall path, including a complete boat's 'heads' (lavatory). Land-mines fell near Manor Park Farm and nearby families were evacuated to the church.

Up the Bosham Channel, Burnes Shipyard was making concrete parts

57 Remains of a landing craft at Combes Boatyard which has now been removed

for the Mulberry Harbours, ready to be assembled off Selsey, with the huge caissons being constructed at Beaulieu and locally at Hayling Island. One caisson that broke its back and never made it to Normandy still lies on the edge of Sinah sands.

Bosham and Chidham suffered from their proximity to the Thorney Island target of German aircraft. ARP diaries record 'Bosham: all posts manned' throughout the summer of 1941: bombs fell, parachutists landed and planes crashed. On 8th October 1940, Mrs Baxendale rang at 20.45 to report a plane down in Chidmere garden and on fire, four men safe but one injured. This seems to have been a favoured spot, for at 06.20 on 3rd

58 D-Day Memorial Service held each year at Itchenor

February 1941, Mr Baxendale reported a plane crashed and three crew inside. In August 1942 the diary records 'Jerry plane machine-guns Southbourne and Chidham, local guns open up...Red Alert...'. Two days later a big midnight raid demolished houses between Bosham and Southbourne. This 'unwelcome attention' was intended for Thorney Airfield. Desperate efforts were made at disguise: 'hedges' were painted across runways and decoy lights planted across Nutbourne Marshes at great cost - their thick cables can sometimes still be found preserved in the mud. One of the worst tragedies to occur at Thorney was on 29th September 1941. A Hudson bomber slewed off the runway and caught fire. The Station Commander and seven others raced out to rescue the crew, the plane exploded and all eight were killed. They never knew that the crew had got clear and were unharmed. There was a distressingly high accident rate overall and RAF losses in 1941 were exceptionally heavy. Wing Commander Douglas Bader's 219 Squadron was decimated and he himself was brought down on a sortie over France. He proved to be a most troublesome POW! However, 219 did have its successes: two Heinkel III bombers were shot down, two crew parachuted down into Chichester - and were taken prisoner. Many air-crew were recovered from the water by the RAF Air/Sea Rescue launches, which had speeds of up to forty knots.

Jack Lewis ran a yard at Emsworth. He was involved with the decoy lights on the marshes and also salvaged aircraft. Across from Emsworth, at the northern tip of Hayling Island, were the Royal Marine and RN bases, HMS Northney I, II and III. Hayling suffered badly from its vulnerable position between two prime German targets: Thorney and Portsmouth. During one especially heavy raid in 1941 over one hundred bombers dropped their loads from 21.00 to 04.00; on Hayling nine civilians were killed and thirty injured. All six gun crew of 219 Battery were killed; there is a plaque at Sinah to commemorate them. Women's Royal Army Corps girls came to man the anti-aircraft positions and many were billeted in draughty Nissen huts without hot water or heating. The girls at Sinah claimed to have seen the first Doodlebug of the war passing over - to explode in the Portsmouth area.

The south-eastern tip of Hayling Island housed the Most Secret of all establishments. COPP

59 COPP canoeist - note mast with light attachment used for signalling

(Combined Operations Pilotage Parties) was based in what is now Hayling Island Sailing Club: a band of adventurers who had volunteered for 'Special Service' without being told what this involved! Here the fifty-seven officers and men, expert canoeists, swimmers and survivalists, trained in all weathers in strictest secrecy. Like the famous 'Cockleshell Heroes', their targets were those impossible for conventional attack and usually so dangerous that a COPP mission was regarded as 'a one-way ticket'. COPPs specialised in the unorthodox - and on many occasions it worked. Midget submarines, or X-craft, 50-ft long, 6-ft wide, displacing thirty-tons, were crewed by COPPists. Packed together inside were diesel engines (two Gardiner or Perkins), an electric motor, air compressor, batteries, escape compartment-cum-heads and canisters to 're-cycle' foul air. Then there was the crew and their gear, all the navigation and signalling instrumentation, food, water - every inch of space held some piece of equipment, some lever or wheel. For the cramped men, keeping silence during a mission meant no movement: the hull plating was only $3/8$ inch thick: in fact the crew could hear German 'asdic' - supersonic soundwaves for underwater detection - pinging off their hull, time for evasive action!

X-craft of the 12th Submarine Flotilla played a vital role on D-Day in June 1944; they were to guide in the first assault boats to the correct landing areas of Sword and Juno beaches in Normandy. COPPists on an advance recce, using canoes, had secured samples from these beaches which proved the ground suitable for the advance-guard's heavy tanks. Canoes used were 'folbots' and could carry 480 pounds in weight; a tiny sail of camouflaged parachute silk could be hoisted on the mast, whose other function was for mounting a powerful signalling lamp.

60 COPP canoes were taken by submarine to within paddling distance of their target area

Lt George Honour, RNVR, had been briefed (most unusually) about the D-Day COPPs mission three weeks in advance. Such was the degree of secrecy demanded that he dared not go for 'a run ashore' during that tense waiting period. He was to command X23 with a Sub/Lt and an Engine-Room Artificer as crew, but taking two extra men as navigation experts. This made for much increased discomfort in the tiny vessel. X23 was ordered to sail on 2nd June, and was towed towards the French coast. Here the midget submarine was submerged for 17 hours 59 minutes. This detailing of the EXACT length of time indicates the ghastly strain of prolonged inactivity in confined quarters and foul air. On 3rd June they moved cautiously to within one-and-a-half miles off the beach, and checking their position through the periscope found they were 'spot-on' - and German soldiers could be seen playing on the beach! Expecting 5th June to be D-Day, the X-craft thankfully surfaced after a further twelve hours underwater, to await their coded message via the BBC. Nothing. In great anxiety they tuned in again at 01.00: 'Invasion postponed 24 hours'; this meant an extra 24 hours of hell waiting on the bottom. At 04.45 on 6th June they surfaced for action and flashed the guiding lights for the in-coming armada as planned; the crew watched landing-craft forging ahead to the beach and our troops swarming down the

61 X-craft, showing the accepted method of conning - without a periscope. The CO rests his arms on a mast to which he was strapped

ramps to wade ashore, ant-like on the great sweep of sand. The job done, X23 turned away for its rendezvous with HMS *Largs*; this proved the most dangerous time of the whole operation. Vessels of every kind were charging towards the shore - nothing should stand in their way now - least of all a tiny, barely visible midget submarine! (NOTE: X-craft were not used to mark the way in for American assault craft, and some missed their correct beach-landing area by a whole mile.)

If the security surrounding COPP was exemplary, so too was it around the harbour villages. Few inhabitants knew exactly what was going on - even at Itchenor, where the shipyard was one of the biggest and busiest. Beyond the harbour, seaward beaches were protected against the possibility - very strong in 1940-1 - of invasion. Steel scaffolding and barbed wire were visible, but 'Other Things' were buried and the waters patrolled by RAF and RN launches. In the harbour mouth a boom defence patrol-boat was sunk near the bar. The *Francis and James*, a Looe fishing-smack, was chopped up under RN requisition and sunk in strategic spots inside the harbour. From 1941-4 the Canadian 1st Army was in charge of Sussex coastal defence, the largest force of Commonwealth troops ever quartered in the UK at any one time. Emergency coastal defence batteries were hastily installed. These were seven miles apart along the coast and operated two 6-inch breech-loading guns which could target ships seven miles offshore. These positions were covered by camouflage netting and manned, initially, by the TA. The eight Home Guard battalions of West Sussex helped patrol these anti-landing defences.

Exercise Fabius on 4th May 1944 was a full-scale rehearsal for the intended Normandy landings a month later. It was realistic in every way - even to casualties: thirty died. The three Assault Forces, British and Canadian, were marshalled, embarked and landed on three coastal sections. Force G on Hayling, Force J at Bracklesham and Force S at Littlehampton.

At Bracklesham, heavy tanks dragged the beach defences apart and two 'Hobart's Funnies' (Sherman tanks with front-fitted arms for exploding mines harmlessly) charged straight ahead and demolished seven seafront bungalows! There were fifty landing craft, two destroyers and two frigates involved and a hospital ship off the Nab was attacked by two Focke-Wulfs, chased off and shot down by fighters from Tangmere. The exercise lasted from 05.30 to 11.00; civilians who had been told to stay indoors saw nothing of the action until tanks, lorries and other vehicles gathered along the main Birdham road before their return to base.

No efforts at secrecy could disguise the drone of hundreds of planes and gliders passing over the harbour area on the night of 5/6th June. From Thorney, four squadrons of Typhoons were dispatched to disable German armour; more from Westhampnett (now Goodwood Airfield) were to target their defensive positions. From Apuldram, three squadrons of Spitfires flown by Czech pilots were to provide cover for the beaches; they flew more sorties than any other RAF station that day. The RAF Ops Room, the HQ controlling fifty-six squadrons, was in Bishop Otter College, Chichester. So efficient was the security blanket that civilians had to listen to the wireless for news, though all who heard or saw the throbbing procession of Dakotas, Fortresses, Lancasters, Liberators, Lightnings, Mosquitoes, Mustangs, Spitfires, Thunderbolts and Typhoons must have known that 'the balloon had gone up' and marvelled at the might of our forces en route to give the Huns 'what-for'. An Itchenor resident recalls seeing an endless queue of vehicles filled with thousands of troops along the main road from Chichester to Birdham and right down to Itchenor Hard. Landing craft of all kinds had been anchored along the Itchenor Reach to Westlands and up the Langstone Channel (some of the heavy anchor chain is still in service for moorings today). During the afternoon of 5th June the vehicles rumbled forward, troops embarked, landing craft moved alongside the special jetty from the tarmac of the road-end to the water, loading and pulling away immediately to keep up the steady flow, unchecked for time was short. H-Hour on Sword Beach was 07.25. Amazingly by 07.30 the first troops were ashore, amongst them the 5th Battalion King's Regiment, embarked at Emsworth. Some unfortunate troops from further afield had been embarked before the bad weather caused postponement and spent seventy-two hours - seasick and cold - in the Channel; they at least must have been thankful that the waiting was over and their landfall was imminent when they saw the coast of Normandy appearing.

So arrived at its destination 'the greatest Armada the world has ever seen'. There were 4,200 landing ships and landing craft, over 1,200 merchant vessels, 1,000 warships and immense air-power to protect those on the ground as well as 1,078 planes and gliders carrying airborne troops. Remnants of that supreme effort can still be seen around the harbour, an area which played a very active part in the build-up towards that decisive moment called D-Day, and was host to the many thousands who gathered, passed through and fought.

62 Canadians on board a Landing Craft Assault during Exercise Fabius in preparation for D-Day 1944

42

The First World War 1914-1918

The First World War - The Great War - played its gruesome part in local history. A study of its memorials gives a sombre reminder of the effect this war had on small rural communities and shows that a high proportion of men made the ultimate sacrifice.

Before the Great War there had been leisure activity around the harbour with regattas and racing increasing in popularity. At the onset of war these activities ceased, and many of the local young men joined the Royal Navy. The older men and boys continued fishing, but boats could only be used with a permit and many areas of the harbour were 'off limits'.

Air power was becoming an important weapon of war and the skills and tools to produce the wooden components were to be found in the local workshops. Tom Sopwith established a small factory at Chidham, and at Emsworth's Queen Street flourmill, plywood components were produced. Much to the amusement of local onlookers, locally produced aircraft were tested there.

Many small airfields were situated along the south coast, being near to the combat area on the continent. An airfield was laid out at Southbourne and American pilots were trained to fly British heavy bombers to attack Germany. It was incomplete at the time of the Armistice in 1918, too late for operations to be put into action.

Many of the district's large houses took in the wounded for recuperation after hospital treatment. Temporary Red Cross hospitals used Langstone Towers and Northlands House at Emsworth as a base. A Prisoner-of-War camp for German prisoners was established at Chichester, and under the terms of the Geneva Convention prisoners were given employment working on local farms.

During the Great War large hydrogen-filled airships patrolled the English Channel observing movements of German U-Boats and fast small craft.

63 Remains of a German U-boat just east of Langstone Mill, 1923

Chapter 5

Of Sailors and their Clubs

Monika Smith looks at the wonderful opportunities for keen sailors through the activities of the sailing clubs around the harbour

The glorious waters of Chichester Harbour are a pleasure to behold, be it from the crest of a wave or from its shores. On bright summer weekends day-trippers from near and far gaze in awe at the nautical goings on at the many sites around the harbour. Most spectators observe the bustling activities from conveniently placed pubs and tearooms, or watch the pretty scenery from one of the many waterside paths.

In total there are fourteen very active sailing clubs and two berth-holders' associations, all of which are members of the Chichester Harbour Federation.

West Wittering Sailing Club is the only village-based sailing club in Chichester Harbour and open to local residents only.

Some families sailed from the beach at Snowhill early in the 20th century, but it was not until 1950 that the West Wittering Sailing Club was officially formed by Major Ford, John and Jen Covington and Sidney Higgs, eminent surgeon and President of the Royal College of Surgeons. The initial aim was to teach children the basics of sailing and dinghy racing. Today the club boasts about 500 members (including children and non-sailing family members). Most of their boats are kept on the creek and on the green by the hut.

Commodore David Swayne muses on the club's popularity:

65 David Swayne in front of the clubhouse, fondly known as The Hut, situated near Snowhill Creek

We are often asked why our friends in other sailing clubs refer to us as the 'Royal' West Wittering. This is because we enjoy all that Chichester Harbour has to offer to the sailor without the encumbrances of large clubhouses and massive subscriptions! Tatler magazine once famously described the club as 'low key', a description

66 The burgees are arranged clockwise in the geographical order of the clubs around the harbour. Starting at 6 o'clock, being the harbour entrance, they represent:

Chichester Cruiser Racing Club
Hayling Island Sailing Club
Mengham Rythe Sailing Club
Langstone Sailing Club
Emsworth Sailing Club
Emsworth Slipper Sailing Club
Emsworth Cruising Association
Thorney Island Sailing Club
Thorney Island Water Sports Centre
Bosham Sailing Club
Dell Quay Sailing Club
Chichester Yacht Club
Itchenor Sailing Club
West Wittering Sailing Club

that fits our famous hut at the end of Coastguard Lane perfectly.

Our events are, however, far from low key. We can attract up to fifty boats a race during the sailing season, and we always ensure that our 'Points Week' does not clash with Cowes, as it is becoming a must for the sailing calendar. Races are staged off East Head sand spit that protects the tidal inlet of Snowhill Creek, where we keep our boats. Start lines are set using our equally famous Committee Boat, a converted Wayfarer, sporting a large WWSC burgee and skull and crossbones on the bow.

Itchenor Sailing Club

Until the First World War the waters off Itchenor and Bosham had been considered THE yachting centre of the harbour and many beautiful cruising craft of the era could be spotted there every season. By 1927 the yachtsmen and dinghy sailors of Itchenor started their own sailing club. In 1931-2 they formed a limited company and acquired four small 17th-century cottages, which were converted to form their clubhouse. The original buildings have since been enlarged.

67 The club's dolphi finial

During the last war the club was requisitioned, first by the Army and then by the Navy, when preparing for D-Day landings. When the sailing club was taken over by the Admiralty the subscription to the club membership was reduced to ten shillings (50p). The remaining anti-aircraft gun emplacement is used as a starting platform to this day.

Various improvements and alterations have taken place over the decades and, apart from many other modern facilities, the club now also offers accommodation with fifteen bedrooms. Itchenor is still the only club in the harbour to regularly sail keelboats - Sunbeam, National Swallow and X-One Design, and International 14, Laser 4000, RS200,

68 Chichester Marina **69** Birdham Pool

International 420 and Laser dinghies. It also has a large cruiser section. The summer programme includes a Schools Sailing Championship (420s and Lasers), a Junior Fortnight and Itchenor Points Week. A Frostbite Weekend is arranged in November.

70 Current Commodore Jim Hartley outside Itchenor Sailing Club

Itchenor's Olympic medallists were Peter Scott (1936, bronze, Olympia-Jolle class); David Bond and Stewart Morris (1948, gold, Swallow class); Charles Currey (1952, silver, Finn class); Rodney Pattison and Ian MacDonald-Smith (1968, gold, Flying Dutchman class); Ian Walker and John Merricks (1996, silver, 470 class).

Chichester Yacht Club was formed in 1967 to complement the new marina, or Chichester Yacht Basin, as it was then called. The present clubhouse was opened in 1992. The magnificent setting between Birdham Pool and Chichester Marina, overlooking the tidal lake at the foot of the channel running up to Apuldram, and immediately beside the lock at the entrance to the Chichester Canal, is steeped in the past use of the harbour.

Standing on the promontory of the clubhouse and looking into the setting sun, it is not difficult to conjure up the image of a Roman galley using the tide to ease its way up to the palace at Fishbourne, or even a Viking longboat on a marauding foray. Later trading vessels of all kinds appeared: the stone for the cathedral passed this point and, later still, sailing barges waited to enter the lock and move up the canal into the centre of the glorious city.

The 2,000 strong membership has a family emphasis and is divided into dinghy, yacht and motor sections offering cruising in company programmes for yachts and motor boats of all sizes, in home waters and across the Channel. Activities range from young sailors, learning basic techniques in the club's Optimist fleet on safe water in front of the club, to the far flung ocean racing achievements of honorary member Ellen MacArthur.

Chichester Cruiser Racing Club members love the thrill of keen, friendly racing and plenty of social activities.

The club was formed in 1948 to provide yacht owners who were members of sailing clubs in the Chichester Harbour area with a race programme. Today the club still fulfils the same aim and caters for boats ranging from six to fifteen metres.

We have an active programme throughout the season with both round-the-cans and passage races, including at least one Channel crossing, and a cruise in company. Several open events are run in conjunction with other Chichester Harbour sailing

clubs. The season starts at the end of April and runs through to the end of October with racing about two weekends a month.

Many take part for the fun of it, while others compete at the highest levels with recent notable successes in RORC races, Cowes Week, Cork Week, the IRC Nationals and the Island Sailing Club's Round the Island Race.

The buzzing atmosphere at Dell Quay on a bright summer's day is quite remarkable for such a tiny place. To think that this was once one of the most important ports in England is hard to imagine. **Dell Quay Sailing Club** is a friendly family club run by its members. They organise regular racing and cruising rallies.

Our clubhouse and dinghy park are situated on the upper reaches of Chichester Harbour next to the small village of Apuldram. The tidal harbour offers the sailor a variety of conditions from the more enclosed waters found at the tops of the channels to more challenging conditions near the open sea. The harbour provides an excellent sailing area in its own right, and a convenient starting point for longer voyages. The harbour entrance is about seven miles from Dell Quay by water.

Our club was established in 1925, and has over the years produced more than its fair share of National and International class competitors. In the 1950s, it was home to a fleet of Sharpies, able to lie on drying-out moorings.

We have a full programme of club sailing and host open meetings for various classes, including Laser, Topper and Enterprise dinghies. Everyone is encouraged to take part in the racing programme, but we also recognise and fully support non-competitive

Views at Dell Quay

recreational sailing and have a programme of cruises and rallies for both dinghies and cruisers. Youngsters are particularly encouraged through our junior fleet, and a training week is organised each summer.

The club has berthing spaces for a large number of dinghies and a small number of (drying) moorings for yachts. There are also many commercial moorings at Dell Quay, and a marina nearby. The Quay itself, now with a pontoon alongside, and our jetty, offer convenient loading for cruisers, both with fresh water available. Our cruising members have a very active programme, with rallies and events throughout the year.

Bosham Sailing Club was founded in 1907 and occupies a unique and beautiful position on Bosham Quay on the north-east side of Chichester Harbour. The clubhouse is a converted water mill, the origins of which date back to 1300, but despite the antiquity of the setting it is a forward looking club with over 1,800 members.

A fleet of over seventy classic day boats, with thirty-three different types based at Bosham, might quite possibly be the largest of its kind racing together in the United Kingdom. Some have been there since the 1930s and their fascinating history has been gathered and recorded by members of the club.

Former Commodore Mike Payne adds more history:

The original club headquarters was established at 'Paddy's Studio' in Bosham and its members were local fishermen and recreational sailors. The club suspended its operations during the two world wars but members revived activities quickly. After 1918, founder and first President, Captain Collis-Chapman MC, remained a continuous and active member of the club for almost fifty years. In those early days the club operated from three locations – Bosham, Cobnor and Itchenor.

In 1947 the ex-MTB (formerly MGB) 614 was purchased and moored against the Quay and served as the clubhouse until 1955, when it had to be removed. By this time, club membership had trebled and larger premises were needed. MTB 614 was sold to the Sea Scouts, towed to the Thames, and moored off Tower Bridge.

73 Mike Payne in front of Bosham Sailing Club

In 1955 the Committee negotiated a long lease of the Mill House from the Earl of Iveagh, Lord of the Manor of Bosham. Alterations were made to the Mill and in 1956 the club moved in. We later acquired the adjoining cottage and garden, which was converted into a patio and terrace.

For many years Cobnor, the use of which we owe to the generosity and kindness of the Beale family, has been an important place for the club. It is home to the popular 'Junior Week', which started in the mid-1960s.

Dinghy races are started and finished there when tide conditions are unfavourable at the Quay. In 1972 a long felt need was fulfilled when the club erected the Pavilion and toilets at Cobnor at a cost of £4,000. Membership had reached 1,600.

In 1973 we became twinned with the Société des Regates du Havre, a famous French sailing club, which was founded in 1838. Annual visits are organised for the cruisers, with one club hosting the other in alternate years - a highlight of the club's programme.

Rear Admiral Percy Gick, CB, OBE, DSM, DSC & Bar (1913-2001)

has written fondly of his Emsworth memories:

At Emsworth there are two sailing clubs. When I arrived there in 1928 the Emsworth Sailing Club also acted as a refuge for the Guards Regiment, one of its early commodores had been Lord Louis Mountbatten and tradesmen were not admitted. Tradesmen therefore formed their own club, the Slipper Sailing Club. They had no clubhouse but they owned by far the most expensive and best boats, some beautiful 18-ft open boats owned by Mr Treagust the butcher and Mr Parham the boat-builder and many other such worthy characters.

I first joined the local sailing club as a cadet in 1928, owning a 16-ft boat which was grossly over canvassed and raced unsuccessfully because it tended to capsize.

During the Second World War Lt Gick flew Swordfish aircraft and was involved in the hunt for the German battleship *Bismarck* in May 1941. He was the only one of nine pilots to score a torpedo hit and subsequently received the DSC for his part in the action. He served on the *Ark Royal* when it was torpedoed by U-81. For his actions Gick was mentioned in dispatches twice.

After the war he served in Hong Kong on the staff of the Commander-in-Chief. On his return to Britain as a Commander, he served on the staff of the RN Tactical School and went to sea in the carrier *Vengeance* as Executive Officer.

In 1952 he was promoted Captain and took command of the destroyer *Daring*. Later as Captain of the aircraft carrier *Bulwark* he towed the burning tanker *Mailika* behind the

aircraft carrier to Muscat in the Oman, thereby achieving the largest ever salvage award for the Royal Navy.

Rear Admiral Percy Gick lived in Bosham but was always very closely associated with Emsworth.

When he retired from the Royal Navy in 1964, he bought the logging pond at the end of Slipper Lane and from it created Emsworth Yacht Harbour which he personally ran until his final retirement in 1991.

75 Emsworth about 1928 with the logging pond at bottom left

76 Langstone Mill **77** Emsworth Marina

In 1992 the club became a limited company and major enhancements were made to the clubhouse at a cost in excess of £200,000. The club is still run by the members for the members with the help of a permanent staff of five.

Thorney Island Sailing Club is a Royal Air Force sailing club formed at the end of 1945 after Wing Commander Hyde, the Unit Signals Officer, discovered that the Sergeants' Mess had considerable funds from pre-war days. He persuaded the mess to fund the building of eight new Hamble Star dinghies to form the basis of the club, together with three old twelve-square metre Sharpies. Sailing started in earnest in 1946, when the club was granted recognition by the Royal Yachting Association and joined the Chichester Harbour Federation.

TISC remained active right up until the closure of the Royal Air Force Station on Thorney Island in 1976. However, two years earlier, in 1974, the then Defence Land Agent, Lord Strathspey, had notice of the possible closure of the RAF station and offered TISC a twenty-one year lease to continue to operate as a sailing club. The RAF Sailing Association agreed that TISC could remain as an Associated Member Club, a situation pertaining to this day. The original lease was agreed in 1976 and subsequently renewed in 1987. Whilst the club is open to personnel from all three services, both serving and retired, it also has a number of elected, civilian, members.

Thorney Island Water Sports Centre is open only to serving and ex-members of the Armed Forces and Ministry of Defence employed civilians.

Emsworth Cruising Association was formed in 1966 by a group of boat owners based in Emsworth Yacht Harbour. Rear Admiral Percy Gick opened the Yacht Harbour in 1965 and wanted a yacht club independent from the harbour organisation. In the early days there were twenty Kingfisher 20s in the Emsworth area and fun races were held between boat owners.

Although the membership has increased and is now much more widely spread, Emsworth is still our focal point. Our main objectives are to enjoy sailing safely for fun and to encourage the newcomer to cruising. Racing has a low priority - although we do support and contribute to events organised by neighbouring clubs. We encourage sailing in company but there is no regimentation; weekend passages generally have a leader, but for advice and guidance only. Route planning and progress during our extended summer cruises tend to be based on group consultation and consensus of opinion.

78 left to right standing: John Burton, Commodore, Malcolm Harman, Rear Commodore Sailing; seated: John R Burton, membership secretary, June Burton, Rear Commodore, Alan Jobson, newsletter editor

79 Emsworth Sailing Club

We have no clubhouse but socialise during the winter at the Emsworth Centre in South Street and hold out-door events during the summer. We have an extensive social and rally programme at home and away. Members receive an informative newsletter for ten months of the year.

Emsworth Sailing Club was inaugurated in 1919 in the former Bathing House on the shore of Emsworth Harbour at the end of Bath Road. Lord Louis Mountbatten was Commodore of the club in 1931, then Admiral for its Golden Jubilee year in 1969, and for the Diamond Jubilee in 1979.

It has seen successive generations of member families make use of its facilities. With a dinghy park for 375 dinghies, and club-owned cruiser moorings, it provides a venue and a base for a wide range of sailors.

Supervised by their parents, young children learn to sail, moving up into competitive sailing in weekly races and more particularly in the Junior Regatta during the summer holidays. Adult member dinghy racing is arranged in conjunction with neighbouring clubs, and is a central feature of the club's sailing programme for the whole family. Picnic outings and other social sailing events are also included.

Rallies and races are organised for the cruiser fleet, of which the furthest afield is the annual rally to St Vaast near Cherbourg. Club members, of course, take their boats much further, recent destinations on voyages from Emsworth including St. Petersburg, harbours in Turkey, and across the Atlantic to Antigua.

Emsworth One Designs have been recorded in use as early as 1895; by 1927 the Lloyds Register of Yachts listed fifty-four of the One Design and Restricted Classes. Each design evolved from the needs and traditions of the waters it sailed. The more successful designs became widely known and copied, including the Sharpie.

Different club boats were being custom-built by local boat builders over the years, amongst them Fowler boats, the Feltham boats and the Parham boats. As lighter, modern dinghies became more popular the club decided to sell its boats in 1962.

The club prides itself in a huge and distinguished membership, perhaps after Lord Mountbatten, the other legendary name being that of world champion, the late Sir Peter Blake, who was tragically murdered by pirates in the Amazon in 2001.

Emsworth Slipper Sailing Club has cruiser, dinghy and junior sections covering all activities. Sail training sessions are held on the Mill Pond.

Member Clive Frost, author of the delightful publication *In Search of a Slipper* sums up the club's history:

Les Pine, our President, charted the years prior to the First World War, when a group

54

of local businessmen, keen to race local boats, organised themselves into the Emsworth Sailing Committee. This activity was suspended during the war but re-commenced soon after.

The history of Emsworth Sailing Club contrasts considerably with the rather itinerant Slipper, which dates from its formal founding on 26th September 1921 as Emsworth Mud Slippers Sailing Club. It had no proper home of its own until January 1963, with the purchase of the Anchor, South Street.

More remarkable then to chart the last seventy-five years of Slipper and celebrate the strengths and differences of both Emsworth sailing clubs, now firmly established on the two prime harbour sites in the town. Long may the strong links remain and the close rivalries spur us all on for the good of sailing.

80 Julian Mandiwall, Commodore, with Emsworth Slipper Sailing Club in the background

Langstone Sailing Club was first formed in 1946, and now has approximately 500 full members, plus two main groups of associate members - IBM, and Langstone Sailability. Originally the club had its headquarters across the road at the Ship public house, but moved to its present site when the toll system on Hayling Road bridge ended.

Sea access to the club on the Langstone side was formerly subject to negotiating a swing bridge for the Hayling Billy rail line from Havant, and the turntable towers and Victorian concrete supporting blocks are still present, forming a useful breakwater in rough weather, while allowing boats passage in between.

The club has a strong dinghy racing tradition, inherited from one of its founder members, Sinbad Zillwood Milledge, the inventor of the Portsmouth Yardstick system for handicapping racing boats, in use worldwide. However, membership is split almost equally between cruising and racing members.

The actual Yardstick is a slide rule and still in the keeping of the club, having been preserved by the Milledge family. They also presented a trophy in his name, which is sailed for each year as an individual and club team event between all Langstone Harbour clubs. By tradition, the trophy remains at Langstone, but is engraved with the winning team's name. The club has enjoyed a long-term association with IBM. Their members, who form an affiliated section within the club, work mainly at the company's North Harbour site, about five miles away to the north of Portsmouth. The section keeps about ten boats on site, Wayfarers, Lasers and Toppers, and joins in club racing and social events as well as organising their own training and open days.

Dr Alec Brennan, Hayling's local doctor, formed **Mengham Rythe Sailing Club** in

1950. He was a very keen sea angler and kept his motor launch in Mengham Creek on moorings rented from Cole Brothers of Salterns Quay. He called a meeting of other creek users with the idea of forming a club, having first ascertained that the vacant timber building (the former clubroom of Hayling Island Sailing Club) was available.

The meeting agreed to form a club to be called the Mengham Rythe Fishing and Sailing Club and to be open to interested boat owners of moderate means. The first commodore was Dr Brennan with the owner of the property, Rear Admiral Ralph Fisher DSO, accepting the position of President. The annual rent was £50.

After ten years or so the fishing side was dropped as more people came into sailing. About the same time, Rear Admiral Ralph Fisher decided to move from Hayling Island and the club was offered Coles Quay and associated buildings and sixteen acres of marshland, including old oyster beds, for the sum of £6,000. By raising loans from members and the bank, the property was purchased.

In 1973 a new and larger timber building was erected by the club members on the same site to cater for the growing membership. Then the club was offered the chance to purchase the tidal mooring areas of Mengham Creek plus mudland bordering the club boundary from the estate of the late Captain Ivan Snell, a fine supportive family to the island. We were pleased to purchase these tidal areas as it gave us protection and secured the future and safety of our seventy or so moorings for our cruisers and dinghies.

The burgee for the club depicts the green ground of Tourner Bury Wood opposite the club where an ancient encampment is known to exist. The heron in flight is because of the heronry in the woods reputed to have been mentioned in Domesday Book. The oyster management and salt panning carried on here, as well as an experiment to extract gold from the sea, can be found in The King Holds Hayling *by Major FGS Thomas and Charles Longcroft's* Hundred of Bosmere. *In spite of all the improvements that have gone on since 1950, the club still holds dear the founders wish: 'A club for all of moderate means'!*

Their splendid new clubhouse opened in 2003 and offers the most up-to-date facilities.

Hayling Island Sailing Club is the UK's leading dinghy sailing club, occupying a magnificent site at the entrance to Chichester Harbour. Founded in 1921, the club has played a premier role in British sailing, encouraging innovation and development, hosting Olympic, national and world class events, and nurturing many generations of sailing champions.

It is sited on a sandy peninsula with direct access to two superb sailing areas; either the sheltered water of the harbour or the open water of Hayling Bay. It is an ideal venue for national and international championships. At high tide it is possible to lay an Olympic course adjacent to the sailing club.

In March 2003 HRH Princess Anne opened the new clubhouse, recognising HISC as a premier location for sailing in the UK, and a RYA Centre of Excellence.

82 Mike Baker, Senior Trustee of HISC and Chairman of Chichester Harbour Federation, at the clubhouse which offers world-class facilities

Four new exciting training schemes have recently started to provide a wide range of opportunities: a programme for children new to sailing; a Local Affiliation Programme; the Duke of Edinburgh Award Scheme; a Pathway to Excellence Programme. Embarking upon these initiatives, the club is proud of its achievements, which includes numerous National, European, and World Champions and five Sydney 2000 Olympic medallists. The view is that success breeds success and young sailors and local school children will undoubtedly benefit from the new programmes.

83 View from Sparkes Marina across to Hayling Island Sailing Club

84 COPP reunion at Hayling Island Sailing Club in March 1977 (left to right) Mike Baker, Commodore Hayling Island Sailing Club; Nick Goodyear, COPPist; Captain Nigel Clogstoun-Willmott, COPP Commanding Officer of HISC, 1939-45; Admiral of the Fleet, Earl Mountbatten of Burma; Jane Baker

In the 1950s and '60s (according to reminiscences by Jim Norris), boats were all wood and often heavy, jambing cleats were not common and of bad design, and cotton sails (no Terylene yet), when wet from a capsize or, more likely rain, meant you had a lot of extra weight just where you didn't want it.

At that time Chichester Harbour Federation would arrange races at East Head every two or three weeks, when the tide was low at mid-day. On these occasions no other club would put on its own races. Boats arrived at East Head going down the harbour on the morning ebb tide and after lunch raced in the various classes.

The Federation had a shed nestling in the sand dunes where tables and chairs and multi-coloured poles and guys (to form a start/finish line) were kept for the race officers and their assistants. From late afternoon it was then possible to sail home on the flood tide.

Representing all the clubs of the harbour is the **Chichester Harbour Federation**.

The need for a regulating body to oversee navigation marks and organise racing had been realised as early as the 1920s. A Joint Committee of sailing clubs makes up the Federation which meets and discusses their interests and needs, sets rules and standards, and acts as a guardian and watchdog over all boating affairs. Affiliated since 1950 to the Royal Yachting Association, the Federation works hand in hand with Chichester Harbour Conservancy. It also holds the largest dinghy event of the harbour season, the record-breaking Chichester Harbour Federation Week.

The Federation's recent Code of Conduct, designed to reduce the conflict between the racing fleets on the harbour and other harbour users, and the racers themselves, has already proved a success. There have been fewer incidents involving racing craft since the code was adopted, and the harbour has become a much safer place. The Federation promotes safe conduct and good manners between all harbour users.

85 Members of Chichester Harbour Federation: left to right (seated): Robert MacDonald, James Davis, Mike Baker, Peter Taylor, Anne Rezin; (back row): David Swayne, Peter Trubshawe, Nick Rizzi, Nigel Pusinelli, Geoff Coop, Hugh Caldwell, Sir Jeremy Thomas, Roger Bleasby, John Sagues

For residents and visitors alike, the harbour is a hugely popular place in which to live, work and relax. There really is a sailing club suitable for everyone, whether a dinghy sailor, cruiser or powerboat enthusiast. Regattas, open meetings and races, all organised by the clubs, add to the colour and life of Chichester Harbour. It is a precious gem for an island nation whose seafaring past has played such a major role in its history.

Chapter 6

Of Birds and Bees

Richard Williamson discusses the causes behind some of the changes that have occured to the wildlife of the harbour over the past hundred years

One hundred years ago, Chichester Harbour was no more than an open air, self-sustaining farm, from which free-range wild birds and their eggs, fish, shellfish and edible plants could be harvested by anyone who found such employment necessary. It had always been so. Stone Age tribes had speared, netted and shot with arrows, this wonderful assortment of salty food, as had the Celts, Romans, Jutes, Saxons, Vikings and later hunters without any major restriction. That is until the moment a century or so ago when some birds were protected and could no longer be killed. It was a shock to a culture that had never experienced such radical ideas in millennia, and some old-timers almost refused to believe that their liberties had been curbed.

With the invention of guns, killing birds had become easy and highly rewarding for the many hundreds of local people in the shore-side villages whose out-of-season jobs could include salt, gravel and sand winning, land reclamation, farming or crewing of boats.

Killing shore birds had been given sport status with the romantic name of wildfowling, when gentlemen gunners like Colonel Peter Hawker (whose 1803-53 diaries are still in print), discussed and enjoyed carrying out daring, daily raids on the swans, geese, ducks and waders in south coast harbours. Double-barrelled punt guns could throw out almost a pound of shot from each barrel.

The exciting craze became so popular that towards the end of his life, Hawker had become shocked by the numbers of 'cockney tailors and pipit poppers behind every bush or afloat in washing tubs', who had ruined his sport and cleared the harbours of birds.

Just over a century ago, a successor by the name of

87 Kingdom Murrell wildfowling in Langstone Harbour

88

Lewis Clements, writing under the pen-name 'Wildfowler', enthused thousands more sportsmen in the cities with his tales of fishing and shooting in the south-coast harbours. This is how he described Chichester Harbour:

For shooting, this harbour is very good. From West Wittering down to the East Pole Sand I have seen a thousand birds at least during the frosty weather. The usual shore birds also abound here. The best places to put up at would be West Itchenor or West Wittering. At either of those villages, boats and men are easily procurable. The harbour is tolerably well sailed about in a small boat. The tramping in some parts is perfectly impracticable, except with mud shoes.

89

In other parts the mud bears well. Those shooters who like shore-shooting can walk from Appledram, a distance of five or six miles along the harbour, when at high tide the shore birds will be easily got at.

In this case, 'birds' were swans, geese, ducks and divers, while shore-birds were waders. This peak count in optimum conditions made by Clements over a century ago would today be minimal. In those days the Brent Geese, Wigeon, Eider,

88 White-fronted Goose
89 Canada Goose

Merganser and various divers that made up the main quarry would be far out to sea by day, as much as four miles, flying in only starlight to the mudflats. They were still there half a century ago and I have heard many tales around the coast of how Second World War soldiers in search of food, used to fire at the rafts of birds with machine guns and even at Mute Swans on Thorney Deeps.

Today, we recognise the same broad blue and silver swords of water running into the Coastal Plain as did those gunners of the past, and as did the Romans in their galleys, but we would not recognise the lack of birdlife. Today, a flight of fifteen thousand Dunlin, twisting their silver underbellies in synchrony, is a daily winter high-tide joy for us as these birds come in to roost.

A century ago, a tenth of this number would have been a rare sight and would have assembled a perfect army of gunners afloat and ashore. They were then called Ox-birds, resembling as they did on the mud the activity of real Ox-birds in Africa on the backs of cattle. The name included all the other members of the Sandpiper family as well as the Ring Plover. With maybe half-a-dozen punts afloat at a time, such a 'trip' of birds would be a valuable cash-crop, and after firing 'into the brown', the birds would be in the Chichester and Portsmouth poulterers by dawn.

90

91

92

90, 92 Common Gull
91 Lesser Black-backed Gull

The first bird protection, apart from close seasons for game birds, began just over a century ago with close seasons for most song birds which protected them from being shot, but not from egg collecting, followed by further protection and the setting up of sanctuaries in the Edwardian period.

Apart from the anomalies mentioned, shooting during the two world wars almost stopped and wildfowl increased all over the UK. However, an unrelated problem for wildfowl had already begun to emerge in 1925, and it was to affect the rich harvest of fish taken from the harbour as well.

Trawling the channels for Bass, Eels, Pipefish, Mullet and the swarms of prawns and shrimps which lived in underwater meadows of Eelgrass (*Zostera marina*) had been extremely lucrative. Fish found sanctuary in a lush, dark green, waving forest of leaves. Suddenly a wasting disease began to attack the Eelgrass and within a few years the underwater forests had gone and the fish had no hiding place. Coupled with this disaster was the pollution brought by urban development.

Worst hit by the sudden disappearance of Eelgrass were the Brent Geese, but there is possibly a further twist to their story sixty years ago. Millions of political detainees were interned under the Stalinist regime in Arctic archipelagoes and they may simply have eaten the eggs during summer and rounded up flightless birds during the moult, as Samoyed tribes in the region had done for centuries in a less intensive way.

In 1954 the Brents were fully protected in Britain. By the 1960s they had begun to increase rapidly until Chichester Harbour held 10,000 birds, or roughly 5% of the world population of this dark-breasted race. Though Brent numbers regularly dip and rise again every few years, at the present time their numbers have begun again a slow decline to about 7,000 birds.

With such large numbers and only a fraction of the Eelgrass available, the birds fed on the seaweed *Enteromorpha* which was enriched by nutrients from

93

94

95

64

farm and sewage. Soon they took to flying onto surrounding farm crops and for the first time in their history as a purely maritime species, became classed as a pest. Even so their value to mankind is far greater in a spiritual sense. Daily flights against winter skies give a musical notation in both sight and sound and make a wild chorus of romantic resonance that involves the experience of wilderness.

Even more exciting is the haunting sound sometimes heard on January nights, as a skein of Grey Geese travel on their way from Sheppey to the Avon water meadows. They may stay a day or two on Thorney meadows and in late February be seen again high up in daylight in one grand chevron on their return.

About twenty species of wading birds commonly spend the winter in Chichester Harbour and by 1945 they had become as common as we see today. Some have increased a great deal more. Grey Plover have increased six-fold to 1,700, Oystercatchers doubled to 1,200, Knot went up from one hundred birds in very hard weather to 600 today. There was an unusually high number of Redshank in 1948 though, when 3,000 were seen in the Deeps in September.

This wonderful marsh with its reedbeds and deep channels, soggy meadows grazed by cattle and horses with copses of thorns and oaks, is a place of complete contrast to the rest of the tidal harbour. It has always been a place for rarities, such as Long-billed Dowitcher (Red-breasted Snipe) seen in 1950 and again in 1959; the white rumped (Bonaparte's) Sandpiper of 1959 and the Marsh Sandpiper of 1951. Large numbers of Snipe and Jack Snipe enjoy the damp meadows, a small flock of Greenshank are usually to be found on one particular muddy edge of the Great Deep, and sometimes a score of Little Grebes are to be seen diving in winter around the Deeps' inflow.

Grey Herons and Little Egrets feed across the grazed meadows, a dense gaggle of Brents, like a flock of black sheep, make a buzzing sound as they do at West Wittering car park when they crop the tight sward. The Deeps will show Moorhens and Water Rails shyly peering out of the reedbeds in spring, and what was once the rarest breeding bird in Britain, the Bearded Tit, may be seen swinging like a pendulum from the reed heads, for it now breeds in some number.

The Little Deep, with its easy seawall viewing, is a winter home for Pochard and Tufted Duck, Teal, Mallard and a host of pipits, buntings, warblers and wagtails.

Back in the 1960s there was a proposal to infill the whole marsh with urban waste to a depth of ten feet. It seems unbelievable today when we all appreciate what a superb attraction every last corner of the harbour is to our quality of life. Refusal of such plans, like that for 'Alcancity' - a new development to be built along the old A27 (the present A259) all the way to Chichester in the 1960s; or the city bypass that was to cross Fishbourne Channel just above Apuldram; or the use of the harbour as a hovercraft testing ground, was made easier with the publication of my report under the Nature Conservancy's (now English Nature) name. This detailed all the requirements for wildlife conservation in Chichester Harbour. It drew a new Site of Special Scientific Interest (SSSI) boundary of protection for the area, much of which overlapped the already existing AONB. The report was the forerunner of the *The Birds of Estuaries Enquiry* which rapidly placed scores more tidal areas in the UK under focus for their wildlife value.

93 Redshank at Fishbourne
94 Reed Bunting at Thorney Deeps
95 Brent Geese at West Wittering

Voluntary enthusiasts like Joan Edom who established herself as a warden at the new Nutbourne Marshes Local Nature Reserve, the Chichester Harbour Wildfowlers, as well as waterfowl counters working originally for the Wildfowl Trust, began to place Chichester Harbour even more firmly on the wildlife map among the many other harbour users who had never before been particularly interested in birds, plants and insects.

Very soon in 1973 the area was awarded Ramsar status and then later designated a Special Protection Area (SPA). With the formation of the Chichester Harbour Conservancy, detailed and inter-locking management planning, fitting wildlife into all other uses, would further secure the needs of the 55,000 waterfowl using the harbour's 8,000 acres each winter.

Knowledge of the subject is increasing yearly as voluntary counters examine and map every bit of the harbour at three different states of the tide, the results published in yearly reports by the Wetland Bird Survey Partnership. How fortunate that the team is lead by such enthusiasts as Anne de Potier in Chichester Harbour.

There are natural changes that may threaten, or may enhance, the harbour. Will the sea invade parts of the land in the next hundred years? A century ago Rice Grass (*Spartina* species) invaded the mud flats, so did the Slipper Limpet. East Head's sand dunes, rich with ninety species of plants like Sea Milkwort, Sea Bindweed and Sea Heath, have altered shape from north-west to north-east, but with help from the National Trust, retains its superb salt and shingle marsh.

Pilsey Island, with its winter roosts of Oystercatchers, its unusual plants like Haresfoot Clover and English Stonecrop, changes shape almost yearly. Saltmarsh meadows at Bosham, Itchenor, Fishbourne and Thorney Island may continue with their luxuriant growths of Sea Purslane, Sea Arrow Grass and Sea Aster for the next hundred years, but I can see slight changes there during the past forty years which are almost imperceptible.

For our lives we will enjoy this vast, fertile, breathing organism with all its colours, shapes, birds, fish, insects and plants pleasing each one of us in all its different ways. We watch and plan for its future, improving it daily as best we can as a place for every person to enjoy, and on into the next century and centuries beyond.

96 Fishbourne Channel showing Spartin
97 Fishbourne Meadows
98 Thorney Deeps

96

Chapter 7

A Landscape of Outstanding Natural Beauty

'What happens on the water is intimately bound up with development on the land'; Ruth Tittensor looks at the landscape of Chichester Harbour through the years

Early 1900s

It is early autumn in 1900, and we are standing on a coastal fabric of flat, wet, hedged and ditched farmland with scattered trees and woodland. Here, the Chichester Coastal Plain meets the muddy foreshore of the five tidal inlets of Chichester Harbour, their long sinuous fingers forming fifty miles of shoreline deep into the landscape. These fingers of sea were once freshwater tributaries of the massive Solent River, which flowed east (along what is now the English Channel) in a dry landscape of the still joined-up continent. After the last Ice Age, the tributaries were drowned by the rising sea, leaving low-lying peninsulas intersected by narrow inlets. Smooth contours of white, chalk hills – the South Downs from Portsdown Hill to the Trundle - distantly circle the now-farmed peninsulas and the adjoining waters of the Solent.

Close your eyes. What can we hear?

> **100** Fingers of the sea push into the rich farmlands of the Coastal Plain

The voices of ten or twelve farm workers and the neighing of eight heavy horses all working on foot, reach us across the fields from the neighbouring farm: heavy horses and heavy work for the men harvesting crops. Less distinctly can be heard the same numbers of men and horses from more distant farms. Fowl, as well as ducks and geese are cackling in every farmyard. Cattle, grazing on the saltmarshes, are lowing as they move across the sward. A shepherd calls his dog as they check the South Downs in the autumn fields. Both people and animals are disturbed by gun shots from wildfowlers getting their dinner in the reeds and deep ditches on Thorney Island. Water is trickling along a muddy creek and a ditcher splashes as he starts clearing the overhanging vegetation. A steam train on the London, Brighton & South Coast Railway at Emsworth Station whistles as it sets off, just north of the harbour – maybe with watercress from the local springs at Fishbourne and Warblington on board. The surging of the incoming tide provides a repetitious and seductive background to the busy, working landscape.

By 1915, the same evocative noises gladden the day, but small planes taking off from the First World War Cobnor Airfield would frighten the heavy horses and cattle. A horse-drawn reaper-binder and steam thresher then get going in the corn fields, drowning the voices of workers gathered around the loud, humming, machinery, as well as the squeals of mice and rabbits in the increasingly smaller circle of uncut corn. Renting the thresher gives the farmer some early cash. The chatter of flocks of sparrows and finches eating the fallen grain in stubble fields suggests that these little birds will be good eating during the coming winter. Low voices from under trees mingle with the sound of long and steady sawing, a reminder that the harvesting season in the oak woods has come round yet again. A steady chop of billhook against wood signifies men coppicing a woodlot, and making hazel hurdles in a copse. At North Marsh, Cobnor, a woman complains about the long prickles in her hands from cutting gorse for fuel for her bread oven.

101 Land Army girl 'Digging for Victory'

1940s

By autumn 1944, the chugging of an International tractor crawling across the drier fields intrudes upon our ears, and we can also hear women's voices - Land Girls - amongst the remaining farm workers. The sounds of Skylarks ascending, of Grey Partridges croaking and Corn Buntings rasping from fence-posts, remind us that despite 'Digging for Victory', the surrounding farmland supports a rich medley of wildlife. Spitfire aircraft-engines roaring overhead spoil the birds' calls when Polish pilots skim just above the oak trees of Salterns Copse, as they take off from Apuldram Airfield. We can feel the soft Brickearth soil beneath our feet, blown by the wind onto the heavy London Clay, after the last Ice Age. The Brickearth is excellent soil for farming, but the London Clay is about two-feet below the surface, and hollows quickly collect water to form marshes and ponds. The sun still feels warm on the skin in autumn. High sunshine levels here produce a long, nine-month growing season. So the climate and soil of Chichester Harbour are very suitable for plant growth, both native vegetation and crops.

102 Recreational boating grew in popularity in the 1970s

1970s

In 1970, the rough, loud sounds of chain-saws and crash of falling trees cut across the calls of skeins of Brent Geese making for the muddy foreshore at Cut Mill, after their autumn flight from the Arctic. The chain-saw screech reminds us that half-a-dozen years of Dutch Elm Disease have devastated the beauty of mature hedges and trees so characteristic of the Chichester Harbour scene. The falling trees are not being harvested, they are dead. Even when the chain-saws are silent, there is no farmland bird song. Post-war farming, which has produced food mountains has, as a by-product, decimated bird and insect life. The human voices we hear are not farm workers or woodsmen, but hundreds of recreational mariners sailing from Dell Quay or beached for picnics on Pilsey Island. Walkers are enjoying the public rights of way at Itchenor and fanning out on the sand dunes at East Head in their increasing leisure time. The drone of cars making their way down Hayling Island to Sinah beach and down the Manhood to West Wittering beach, is a new and constant noise in a now beleaguered landscape.

2000

In autumn 2000, the voices we hear are still mainly those of leisure-seekers, and a few horticultural workers gathering lettuces – but there are no farm workers' voices. Occasionally workers' voices can be heard, but they belong to rangers mending stiles, or ecologists shouting information to one another across Fishbourne Meadows. Mariners are discouraged from the muddy shores for fear of erosion and disturbance to wildlife. Their talk is concentrated in packed marinas like Northney, which have replaced the working quays of 1900. We can still hear horses, but they are ridden for pleasure, not worked for profit in the fields. Heavy horses are gone. Large numbers of cattle are lowing, maybe two or three times the number of those in 1900 or even 1944. They are in enclosed fields, not the open marshes - which are now quiet, except for a few wildfowl and the tide. The cackle of domestic fowl, ducks and geese in farmyards is absent. Our eggs and poultry come from elsewhere. The sounds of 1900 - of ten farm workers and eight heavy horses per holding - have been replaced by maybe a dozen items of farm machinery on each farm, driven by noisy internal combustion engines. Jets drone high above, while combine-harvesters hum across the golden fields. Their drivers are enclosed in a cab, listening to their digital radios!

There are still the sounds of Brent Geese; their numbers have increased by about twelve times since 1944. But something is not quite the same. Where are the Brent Geese? They can be heard on the farmland, not on the fore-shore! Yes, they are on the farmers' pastures. A small cannon goes off, while a farmer swears, as the cannon fails to intimidate the geese! Their chatter is enjoyed by thousands of visitors all round the harbour: walkers, cyclists, birdwatchers, volunteers planting trees, wheelchair and buggy users.

103 Noisy farm machinery has replaced the heavy horses and farm workers of the 1900

Early 1900s

Now we are back again in 1900. What do we see around us in the landscape of Chichester Harbour? In autumn 1900, fields are full of men and heavy horses steadily working at reaping and stooking the long-stalked corn, or starting on early hedge maintenance. Men have walked from Chichester, Havant and Portsmouth for their day's work. The tall, uncut corn is golden, and bright with wild flowers like Corn Marigold and Field Poppy - this is a time of deep farming depression. Farm incomes are insufficient to pay for hoeing weeds in the fields of roots (mangolds, swedes and turnips), so Fluellen and wild Antirrhinum fill the gaps.

104 Swedes - and horses - were once a familiar sight on local farms

But wild grasses and flowers are an intimate and important part of the ecology and food value of hayfields and pastures. There are even overgrown areas, as at Bosham Hoe, where Gorse, Tufted-hair Grass and Rush are spreading, providing habitat for Skylark and Partridge. We can see a network of flowing and standing open water, reed bed swamp and marsh habitats with Angelica and Yellow Iris between and in the fields. Moorhen, Mallard and Reed Buntings, frogs and Water Boatmen share the farm with cattle and sheep. Chill winter winds, laden with salt, have helped form the hunchbacked lines of trees between foreshore and field. Red Devons and brown Shorthorns graze on the saltmarshes - good for milking at a time when the nearby railway (also brown livery!) can take the milk to nearby towns. A man is collecting luscious Glasswort from the mudflats, an excellent addition to his breakfast.

In autumn 1915, the scene is basically the same, but wartime needs have made farming very profitable and the rough gorse areas are now cultivated. Men are building and thatching straw ricks. Sparrows and finches are darting into the fields and farmyard for the spilled grain. Rabbits are still a dreadful pest, so we might see men out with ferrets and purse nets, long nets and dogs, catching large numbers for export by train to the towns. The coppicers carefully cut back the many-stemmed shrubs in the woods, providing hurdles and firewood for farm use. Mature Oak and Elm are felled with six-foot long, cross-cut saws, needing two men each to wield them, each tree worth a fortune. The foreshore is changing. A new, tough, spiky grass - an immigrant called Cord Grass - is spreading from the west, building up the mudflats, so the Glasswort is disappearing and the coastline changing.

1940s

As we survey the 1944 scene, a good time for farming is following an inter-war depression. Farmers use basic slag from steelworks to fertilize the corn, yet poppies and field pansies still colour the gold. Grass pastures and hay meadows are still embellished by thousands of wild flowers, like Birds-foot Trefoil, adding to their nutritional value. Damp pastures, such as Lighters Field, Bosham, are full

105 Wheat field at Chidham

of orchids. But some pastures have been ploughed and resown with grass-clover mixes (called leys) to increase their productivity. So we notice more cattle per acre. In the fields of roots, flocks of Lapwings rise and call 'peewit', and Brown Hares rush away, as a Land Girl drives by on a new Fordson tractor. Sugar-beet is being harvested. The Oak trees of Salterns Copse look really sad, where they have been cut back to allow the Spitfire pilots more leeway when taking off. The pastures are full of rabbits, whose burrows undermine the fields. Skylarks and Grey Partridges are still abundant in the rough. Ducks dabble in the ponds and Water Voles have left tell-tale holes in the ditch banks. The small, black Brent Geese are eating Eelgrass at low tide level on the foreshore.

1970s

When we open our eyes in 1970, the picture is drastically different. Firstly, the landscape is flatter: hundreds of mature trees have vanished. Dead Elms have had to be felled. The countryside is even a different colour. The short-stalked corn is suitable for the massive combine harvester, with a single machine in summer. By early autumn the stubble has been burned, the fields ploughed and even sown with next year's harvest: thus the landscape is dark-brown, not golden with ripe corn. This change in farm management has had enormous results on the view. There are no flocks of finches and sparrows eating spilled grain or Lapwings searching for insects, because the efficient combine, followed by stubble-burning, has removed their foods. There are no ricks, as now we have huge bales of straw lined up at field edges until sold. No sugar beet, mangolds, swedes or turnips are grown: piebald Friesians, which have replaced Devons and Shorthorns, eat silage, not root crops. The Brown Hares eat nothing - we cannot see hares, or Skylarks flinging themselves into the heavens. Without root crops, rough places or permanent grasslands, Brown Hares cannot find hollows to lie, feed or breed. And summer harvesting by men in machines is too early for Skylarks; it has destroyed their nests.

The grass fields are bright emerald green, but we see no wild flowers! The 'weeds' (wild flowers!) have succumbed to the combination of artificial fertilizer, herbicide and the plough. They have been resown with new strains of Rye-grass which grow large and bright green when artificial fertilizers are added; great for milk production.

Flatter - and drier too. EU grants to drain land have increased the acreage suitable for ploughing and sowing with Rye-grass or cereals. Maize cobs are ripening and fields are packed with tall oil-seed rape. Ponds and marshes have become arable, minus orchids or Wild Angelica. Hedges and foreshore tree-lines are thin, gappy, and shockingly mutilated. The coppices have been abandoned for thirty years; the reeds at the mouth of the River Lavant are brown, overgrown and unused. Apart from intensively managed farmland, habitats in the landscape are abandoned. Even in Chichester Harbour, there is uniformity all around.

As we look down the muddy foreshore of Fishbourne Channel, it too is bright green, with overgrowth of green seaweeds. Artificial fertilizers added to the soft, ploughed fields in winter and spring, have leached into the soil and through to the foreshore where they grow green algae, not cereals! The

106 Weed building up on the foreshore

foreshore is also pock-marked with boat-shaped hollows, where mariners moor their craft. The tide is wallowing around the hollows, eroding the mud. Hardly a farm worker is to be seen, made redundant by machinery and changed farming. Even the rabbit-catchers have gone, as myxomatosis in 1954 cleared out most rabbits.

Looking across Chidham parish, we suddenly spy a brightly coloured phenomenon squeezing through a metal field gate. It is the largest tractor, with the largest wheels, ever seen. Attached behind is the largest plough ever, with its two rows of six plough-shares stuck up into the air. Lowered into the soil, it quickly ploughs six furrows at a time, more than fifteen acres a day. Back in 1900, with horses, it was one furrow at a time, and just one acre a day!

107 Volunteers coppicing the hazel trees at Salterns Copse

Thousands of people are still enjoying themselves everywhere on land and sea in Chichester Harbour. For instance, through hedge gaps, lines of naturalists peer through binoculars, or stoop to search diligently for cornfield weeds still growing at Apuldram. And Chichester Harbour landscape is still incredibly beautiful and rich in wildlife, despite the changes and losses since the Second World War. To stop further losses and ensure renewed beauty and value for the future, the Countryside Commission designated Chichester Harbour as an Area of Outstanding Natural Beauty (AONB) in 1964. This is a national recognition and valuation, from which many positive landscape changes arise in due course.

2000

Thus, as we arrive in autumn 2000, the volatile landscape and coastline have changed yet again. More people are visiting the countryside, walking along Chichester Harbour paths. The dunes are now rounded and complete, with new lines built up seaward with the help of volunteers who have piled palings and brushwood for sand to accumulate. The shepherd's dog has been replaced by a Land Rover or quad bike, whilst family dogs delight in the space and freedom of Hayling Island beaches.

Rangers maintaining the Sussex Border Path and ecologists counting birds along Emsworth Channel or taking soil samples in a woodland, are working in the landscape. Groups of volunteers dig holes and plant small trees at Prinsted. Others are coppicing the hazels of Salterns Copse once more, or spiking themselves on blackthorn and hawthorn as they slot them into hedge gaps. A bunch of school students, with clipboards and pencils, is poking in the mud and counting the shells within the grey ooze.

108 Feeding the Jacob sheep at Cobnor

The only farm worker visible in the landscape is holed up in his tractor cab. There are few hares or Lapwings, though song birds flit around. Brent Geese waddle and puddle in large numbers across the peninsulas, farmers and conservationists generally now in agreement on how best to manage both the landscape and these inhabitants.

Friesians stand in a farmyard, munching at a wall of smelly silage topped with tyres. A huge round container stores the manure that was once so precious to the land's fertility. The 1987 Great Storm has wiped out yet more mature trees along shores and hedges. But 25-feet high clones of Elm stand in the hedgerows along Apuldram Lane, sprouted from their parents' living roots. Beetles refuse to let them grow taller, so their flaking bark and dead branches silhouette the skyline. At Cobnor, there are new ponds in which we can see fish and yes, frogs.

Amazingly, below Prinsted, there are fields where the sea has apparently broken through the sea wall and formed new saltmarsh, yet farmers are not attempting to drain and return it to productivity! This is a deliberately managed haven for wildfowl and waders and a soft form of protection from the sea. A cut reed bed and new reed plantings have sprouted fresh, green growth, to encourage the Reed Buntings.

109 Farmland near Fishbourne

Unfortunately no watercress is for sale from spring-fed beds at Fishbourne and Warblington, as it is no longer economic, and anyway the pure water here has been polluted by run-off from new roads.

Interestingly, though, the only two commercial sites for watercress in Sussex are still in production today. They are not too far from the harbour, at West Ashling and Hambrook, where the beds have been kept in production since the 19th century.

There are rough areas of farmland with gorse, brambles and Tufted-hair Grass: these are called 'Set-Aside'. The name doesn't matter, they are once again used - for wildlife - thanks to new grants from the Common Agricultural Policy. We can see that there are more bushes and willow clumps, as thousands of trees have been planted around the shoreline. A rabbit hops out of a sandy burrow under scrub at Ellanore; myxomatosis is less virulent now.

Habitat variety and landscape amenity have replaced the relative uniformity forged by post-war farming. People in the landscape are not breaking their backs hoeing the fields or plodding all day behind heavy horses. They are enjoying themselves, are learning, and are working for amenity, beauty and ecological variety. Farmers are still working to fill our larders too, but inventiveness and technology mean that less land is sufficient for those needs.

Our tour of the Chichester Harbour landscape emphasises that its farmland and shoreline, its beauty and ecology, have been susceptible to natural events, advancing technology, European politics and social change throughout the last century. The South Downs encircle the harbour a few miles to the north; huge skies can still be seen from the farmlands. Yet the fifty miles of tree-lined inlets are intimate once more; their seventeen miles of sailing waters are safe; there is again a superb variety of natural and human ecosystems. The farmland and woods change from season to season; people work at land-based skills, like farming, conservation and footpaths. The whole landscape mosaic changes from decade to decade. These features all ensure that Chichester Harbour Area of Outstanding Natural Beauty fully deserves its 1964 national landscape designation.

110 At Thornham Point, near Prinsted, the sea has been allowed through the sea wall to create new saltmarsh

Chapter 8

Of the Conservancy

A landscape as precious as this needs strong and effective management in order to survive and prosper; the Conservancy's task is not an easy one, says Monika Smith

Residents have to co-exist with the many-faceted aspects the harbour presents to its important visitors, be they of the human, furry or feathered variety, land or water based. Interests from many differing quarters put pressure on this rural idyll, designated an Area of Outstanding Natural Beauty as far back as 1964, when it had first become obvious that its fragile future was under threat.

Until the Conservancy took over the management of the whole harbour, its administration was divided down the centre of Emsworth Channel between the Hampshire and West Sussex sides. Harmonious administration became increasingly difficult between the two harbour boards on each side of the county boundary. By agreement between all concerned, representations were made for a single, statutory authority to be in control.

In recognition of the importance of good overall administration, the Conservancy was established by the Chichester Harbour Conservancy Act 1971. The three County Council officers, who did the initial work to establish the Conservancy, were Geoffrey Godber, first Clerk to the Conservancy, with David Durbin and Bob Hanson. The first chairman was Vice Admiral Sir Geoffrey Thistleton-Smith, KBE, CB, GM, DL.

112 The Conservancy and Advisory Committee on their annual tour of the harbour in 2003

The Conservancy looks after every aspect of the harbour, its integrated landscape and physical features on land and water, as well as residential and recreational needs. A careful balance has to be struck between

113 Martin Daws-Chew, Chairman of the Conservancy, at Dell Quay

these and nature conservation and the protection of the harbour's natural beauty.

Other responsibilities cover safety of navigation, the regulation of moorings, works and dredging, enforcement of harbour byelaws and the collection of dues and charges. Additionally, the Conservancy has a range of powers under countryside legislation relating to such matters as nature reserves, tree planting, access agreements, car parks, camping and picnic sites.

The Conservancy acts as a Joint Advisory Committee for the Chichester Harbour Area of Outstanding Natural Beauty (AONB) and is consulted on all planning policies affecting the area.

The Conservancy consists of fifteen members appointed by West Sussex and Hampshire County Councils, Chichester District and Havant Borough and the Conservancy's Advisory Committee. The Advisory Committee includes representatives of harbour and amenity area users, such as sailing, fishing, nature conservation, residents', farmers' and commercial interests. The Conservancy must consult the Advisory Committee on the management of the harbour and amenity area.

The post of chairman of the Conservancy is rotated every three years. During his term in office, current Chairman MARTIN DAWS-CHEW acts as the public figurehead of the Conservancy and represents the public interest, operating a system of drawing together harbour users and residents.

Martin was born in Bracklesham during the last war and has lived in the Witterings area most of his life. He is also an elected member of West Sussex County Council, representing the Witterings Ward.

Martin warmed to the satisfying task of being engaged in local democracy and says he could not wish for a better job. Standing by the water's edge and observing the swans processing in the rising tide, he reflects on the beauty and tranquillity of his beloved harbour but adds with caution: 'My main concerns are the rapid development of the south coast and the threat to the harbour area in particular. It is now the largest remaining site of natural harbour still as yet unchanged by commercial interests between Brighton and Southampton and the pressures we are facing are extreme. There is an escalating demand for resources and it will get more difficult to accommodate competing pressures.'

Present Chairman of the Advisory Committee is ROGER BLEASBY, whilst NIGEL

80

PUSINELLI, CMG, OBE, MC, is the representative voice of the Royal Yachting Association. Both men share a great passion for sailing and all matters concerning Chichester Harbour.

In 1958 Roger built his own boat from a kit, so that he could join Dell Quay Sailing Club. He spent many happy years cruising the home waters before getting involved with the committee. Nigel has fond memories of being the Commodore of Aden Yacht Club and sailing in the harbour when on leave. Nigel was also a founder member of the

114 Roger Bleasby (left) and Nigel Pusinelli at Emsworth Sailing Club

Conservancy and has been part of the Advisory Committee ever since. Actively involved in the Emsworth Sailing Club for very many years, he is known locally as the 'Grand Old Man' or the 'Doyen' of Chichester Harbour. Its interests have always been close to his heart. He remembers the days before the Conservancy formation as tricky, with harbour interests always being at risk.

115 John Davis, Harbour Master, by the Conservancy office

Nigel comments: 'Chichester is the first - and only - harbour authority in the country with such tight and efficient management working with so many different factions. Blessed are the days when the Conservancy was formed!'

The challenges of managing an area of such importance with so many potential conflicts are clear. The Conservancy, in its latest management plan for 2004 until 2009, highlights six key concepts: protecting and improving the special qualities of the AONB; sustainability and wise use; increasing knowledge and understanding; helping people to enjoy the AONB; supporting the local community and economy; working in partnership.

At the helm of the Conservancy since 1996 is Manager and Harbour Master Lieutenant-Colonel JOHN Q DAVIS. His staff of twenty help him look after the three main areas of the Conservancy's duties, the harbour, the AONB and general administration.

The administration sets policies, presents issues, liaises and advises. John's role is to govern the Conservancy's work in a democratic and diplomatic fashion. There are as many as sixteen different interest groups with conflicting needs. The Conservancy has to present or suggest a balance to satisfy the common purpose and vision. The team has the task to find ways to exist in harmony with demands from conservation, commercial interests, urban developments and planning, recreation, people pressure, litter, traffic and natural changes like climate, rising sea levels and erosion. They currently work closely with the two County Councils, the Countryside Agency, the Heritage Lottery Fund, English Nature and the RSPB.

Deputy Harbour Master RICHARD CRAVEN, formerly a fishing officer in Wales, has been in post since 1998. He looks after the day-to-day running of the harbour. As the right hand of the Harbour Master, Richard sorts out all the practical work with a team of three, based in the workshop and working from the maintenance boat, *Regnum IV*, a mooring barge with a crane and machinery on board.

116 Richard Craven, Deputy Harbour Master, with *Regnum IV*, **117** Roger Young (standing left) with the patrol team

His team manage navigational aids, harbour lights, hazard warnings, a programme of maintaining buoys, beacons, marker posts, pontoons, jetties and moorings.

Patrol Officer ROGER YOUNG is part of the team collecting harbour dues, ensuring safety, enforcing byelaws and patrolling moorings. Carrying out random patrols throughout the harbour acts as a visible presence during the busy summer period. In 2003 the patrol team was called out for assistance a record number of 174 times. The reasons for call-out ranged from breakdowns, collisions, grounded vessels, on-board fires, sunken boats, oil spills, injured birds and missing people. The odd illegal immigrant is also added to the ever-growing list of alarm calls.

117

Workshop Foreman MIKE 'CHARLIE' WEBB maintains boats and moorings from Itchenor and Prinsted, and often takes the barge, along with the workshop team, 'to work with Sid, our man in Emsworth'. Together they carry out routine checks on markers, buoys, and all the other practical regular maintenance work. Part of the job is to maintain all the moorings before the winter sets in each year.

Charlie's father was a local boat-builder and from boyhood Charlie has kept up the traditional skills. He built his own fishing trawler, *Merlin*, in 1977 - shown on the cover of this book - which he still takes out to sea a few times a week to catch his dinner.

118 Charlie Webb, Workshop Foreman, outside the Conservancy workshop at Itchenor

His counterpart over the water at Emsworth is SYD KENNETT. Syd is the fourth generation of Emsworth fishermen. His little harbour office/workshop stands near the picturesque Town Quay at South Street. Syd is as much a local attraction as the stunning scenery, with locals and strangers constantly stopping for a chat. For the past thirty-six years Syd has been clearing the foreshore, checking the pontoons, or putting salt on the jetties in the winter. The Harbour Conservancy 'inherited' Syd from Havant Borough Council and he has gladly carried on ever since.

119 Syd Kennett, Harbour Hand, outside the tiny Emsworth Harbour Office

Every morning at 7.30 he walks along the waterfront where he meets up with Harbour Master John Davis for a brief update. During the day he checks moorings and assists boating visitors. On weekends he also runs a local ferry service for boat owners. Syd loves his job to such an extent that he rarely enjoys his time off and always looks forward to returning. He knows all, and all know him - and if you can't find him outside somewhere try the Blue Bell pub!

In spring he paints numbers on the 150 or so mooring buoys. Some winter work might also include planting trees elsewhere in the harbour area. Whatever is required out of season, Syd is always on call. He is a real asset to the Conservancy and is equally complimentary about his employers in true colloquial style: 'I loves my work and the Conservancy, they are wonderful folk. Without them the harbour would be a right shambles!'

The Conservancy develops and delivers policies for the management of the AONB.

120 Philip Couchman, the AONB Manager, in his office overlooking the Hard at Itchenor

PHILIP COUCHMAN, the Conservancy's Manager of the AONB, has been in his post for nearly thirty years. Until the late 1980s he worked on his own, setting up programmes and overseeing the growth in legislation. These days a small team assists him with the protection and improvement of the environment. Of specific concern are nature conservation, education, public and press relations and an efficient information service.

Improving the environment involves working closely with the Farming and Wildlife Advisory Group (FWAG) producing 'Whole Farm Conservation Plans' for farms within the AONB boundaries. Nine major farms and smallholdings border some of this land, and any works or changes proposed need the consent of the landowners. Coastal grazing marsh is an important habitat within the harbour, not only for its plants but also for breeding waders. In order for the areas of marsh to remain open and biologically rich, they need suitable levels of grazing - ideally by cattle. Like elsewhere in the country, the number of grazing cattle within the harbour is declining, which raises concerns about the future of these important habitats. A combined project has recently been developed to sell locally-reared beef to local people.

121 A successful project to protect Water Voles was led by the AONB team

The team works towards the protection of endangered species and their habitats. One on-going project is to protect and enlarge the habitats for Water Voles to allow their numbers to increase. The planting of trees and hedgerows is as much part of the work as the production of interpretation boards and a lively website.

Countryside management includes footpath maintenance and the provision of 'Access For All' in this diverse area.

It is a site full of habitats for species of international and national importance, productive farmland, and a very popular holiday destination with valuable housing sites. Conflicts of interest are potentially looming. There is a Conservancy moratorium on further moorings to allow the present dinghies and boats enough space to sail, but also to protect rare plants and wildlife and preserve the tranquillity of the harbour.

The enlarged and improved management team can concentrate its efforts more successfully. On permanent stand-by are also a dedicated volunteer force, the invaluable Friends of Chichester Harbour (with membership of over 2,000), the Chichester Conservation Volunteers, the British Trust for Conservation Volunteers (BTCV), and about forty-five Harbour Watchers. They each look after stretches of the fifty miles of shoreline, picking litter, checking erosion on footpaths and keeping records of findings and changes.

122 Friends of Chichester Harbour volunteer work party, clearing the wheelchair path at Itchenor

The harbour's valuable mudland is never far from the team's mind. Much time in 2003 was devoted to developing the numerous environmental projects within the Rhythms of the Tide Heritage Lottery Fund Project. This work is funded through the County Councils' precept, the Friends of Chichester Harbour and the Countryside Agency.

What of the future? There are changes in climate, global warming, and rising sea levels. Increased affluence brings increased leisure, so the human demands on the harbour will be stretched further, which might conflict with migrating birds. There is a struggle between nature conservation versus recreation. Once there was harmony with birds using the harbour in the winter and yachts in the summer. It is important that they still co-exist in harmony.

123 Anne de Potier, the Conservancy's Conservation Officer

Continuous erosion will have an impact on future access and great pressure is coming from developers. The Conservancy needs to be ever vigilant with encroaching urbanisation, as each change has a knock-on effect. Philip's heartfelt hope is that, despite changes, there will still be great pleasure to be had in the harbour in the future.

Conservation Officer ANNE DE POTIER joined the Conservancy in 1988. Her responsibility is the conservation and enhancement of wildlife in the harbour. Anne's work involves organising research into wildlife, along with habitat and

species protection and their management. A key aspect of the work is collecting data related to the harbour's national and international designations: for example, the monthly counting of waterbirds shows which species (such as Redshank) are particularly important and how their numbers have fluctuated, as well as what management issues need to be tackled.

At Dell Quay is the Conservancy's popular Education Centre, and the newly-refurbished grain warehouse opposite has just been opened as a community centre and meeting place for the sailing club.

Looking after the educational projects and lively activities programme are JOHN TIERNEY, Schools and Community Officer, and JUDI DARLEY, Education Officer. Her family, the Darleys, goes back deep into the harbour's history.

Judi supervises the public in an informal yet effective way, arranging a multitude of activities, appealing to as wide a range of people as possible.

124 Judi Darley organises a whole range of activities for people of all ages to learn about the harbour in an informal way

'Harbour Creekies', informal bi-monthly - child free! - gatherings to learn about the harbour from the comfort of the warm and dry Education Centre, started in 2004. 'Oystercatchers' Family Fun' are monthly sessions designed with harbour themes. Other interesting events happen throughout the year to suit all tastes and age groups. These include the annual 'Paint the Harbour!' day and regular photographic sessions.

John concentrates on the more formal aspects, primarily dealing with schools and the National Curriculum. He visits schools during winter and arranges fascinating field trips around the harbour for school groups throughout the summer. Coaches of children come down to Dell Quay to use the facilities. The Education Centre accommodates up to fifty children and a team of supply teachers is on call to assist with environmental studies. Encouraging local people to look after their inheritance is part and parcel of the job.

125 John Tierney, Education Officer, in his puppet theatre featuring a range of harbour creatures

The school programme and activities are designed to appeal to all tastes. Using creativity, information technology, art, music and dance can make geography and science fun, with themes ranging from air-sea rescue to weather. The living outdoor classroom becomes a natural playground and teaches children the value of affinity with nature. Children love this beautiful place for offering such an inspirational adventure.

Publicity Officer ALI BECKETT is kept busy all year round designing many of the Conservancy's leaflets, booklets including the annual *Chichester Harbour News & Guide* and press releases. Good communication between all sections of the vast harbour community and 'the rest of the world' has never been more important. Any pressing issue can only be effectively addressed if information is forthcoming, fast and accurately.

126 Ali Beckett with pupils from Ealing School and West Wittering Primary School

Judi Darley and Ali Beckett organise and lead many extremely popular guided walks and events around the harbour throughout the year. There is a growing programme of activities published annually, with strong support from the Friends of Chichester Harbour and the Countryside Agency.

Other members of the Conservancy management team include VICKY BLAMIRE, Planning and Property Officer, whose dual roles are advising the Conservancy's Planning Committee on policy and planning applications, and overseeing its legal and property business around the harbour.

ALISON FOWLER, AONB Officer, implements the Management Plan, supervises footpath maintenance and other access issues, works with landowners and captains the Conservancy's Rounders Team in its annual match against the Itchenor Society!

Thanks to support from the Heritage Lottery Fund and other sponsors, the Conservancy has welcomed a fabulous new craft on its waters. As from spring 2004, the solar-powered boat, *Solar Heritage* - imported from Switzerland and only

127 Publicity for *Solar Heritage*, the Conservancy's new solar-powered boat

Chichester Harbour
by **Solar Boat**
Learn about the environment of Chichester Harbour from our solar powered boat 'Solar Heritage'

Solar Heritage
SOLAR POWERED BOAT

Chichester Harbour Conservancy
Area of Outstanding Natural Beauty

128 David Rolph, Chairman of The Friends of Chichester Harbour

the second vessel of its kind in British waters - operates with experienced guides leading educational visits, nature watch, photography and combined walk/boat trips.

THE FRIENDS OF CHICHESTER HARBOUR, with a membership of over 2,000, are an invaluable source of help and assistance. The group is a registered charity solely concerned with sustaining and improving the environment of the harbour for the benefit of all users - both the people and the wildlife.

The group was formed in 1987 to provide a focus for voluntary activities. Sailors, fishermen, walkers, naturalists, wildfowlers, local residents – many of them 'well heeled' and influential - as well as smitten visitors, make up the formidable membership with the united purpose of ensuring the well-being of the harbour.

They work to support the Conservancy in various practical ways, and help financially with donations to care for and improve the harbour environment. They are represented on the Conservancy's Advisory Committee and are affiliated to the BTCV.

They produce a regular newsletter and help with practical outdoor work parties. These projects include planting trees and shrubs, reed-cutting and stream maintenance, litter clearance, coppicing and woodland management, guarding nesting sites, shoreline monitoring, bird surveys and access projects. Others have applied their skills and many talents in producing wonderful items for the Education Centre. Individually designed cushions (some with beautiful tapestries of local scenes) have been made for more comfortable seating. Nimble-fingered ladies also have made delightful puppets and sea creatures for the puppet theatre.

Finally, we come to the CHICHESTER HARBOUR TRUST.

The qualities of natural beauty and tranquillity that make Chichester Harbour so special are increasingly rare in Britain and, as their rarity grows, so will the value of the harbour as a local and a national asset.

In 2003, the Conservancy set up an independent charitable trust to acquire land around the harbour to safeguard it for the future. Ownership being the best form of guardianship.

Working to secure the future of Chichester Harbour

Chichester Harbour Trust

129 The Trust's first publicity leaflet, 2003

CHICHESTER HARBOUR
NEWS & GUIDE
2004

Area of Outstanding Natural Beauty

It has recently been recognised that the only way to safeguard the future of some of the threatened key areas of land, sites and buildings, is through ownership by the Trust, and management by the Conservancy. The Trust was set up to enable fast action when threatened sites come on to the market. It is currently chaired by founder member Sir Jeremy Thomas, former British Ambassador to Greece, a keen sailor and author of the delightful book *The Rhythm Of The Tide: Tales through the ages of Chichester Harbour.*

Thanks to the great enduring love and dedication of the harbour people it has, so far, been possible to stem the ravages of time, weather and progress.

Admired and treasured by all who are caught in its spell, Chichester Harbour must not fall victim to its own popularity. With effective management, and with so many influential people, and so many friends, the harbour *will* have a future. The Conservancy's role as guardian in securing this great future is therefore more vital as ever as the years roll on.

131 The Harbour Office, the Conservancy's waterside home at Itchenor

Picture Credits

Copyright is vested in the respective owners

Michael Austen, 29

Mike Baker, 84, 85

Doreen Bennett, 5

Marguerite Bettles, 101

Lady Pippa Blake, 26

Chichester Harbour Conservancy, 23, 57, 58, 63, 64, 100, 102, 106, 112, 115, 117, 123, 127, 130

Chichester Harbour Federation, 66

Chichester Harbour Trust, 129

Chichester Observer, 126

Countryside Agency/Terry Heathcote, 30, 38, 39, 49, 55, 97-9, 103, 105, 107-10, 122

Charles Currey, 28

David Darley, 8

Emsworth Marina, 75

Brian Fellows, 121

Alan Gick, 74

Trevor Glanville, 52

John Groves, 13

Jim Hartley, 70

Havant Museum, 27

Bill Kentell, 10

Langstone & District Wildfowlers Association, 87

Charles Pears, 25

Basil Rizzi, 21

Royal Marines Museum, Southsea, 59-62

Matt Simmons, 24

Monika Smith, 1-4, 6, 7, 9, 11, 12, 14-20, 22, 31-7, 40-8, 50, 51, 53, 54, 65, 67-9, 71-3, 76-83, 111, 113, 114, 116, 118-20, 124, 125, 128, 131

Roger Smith, end papers

West Sussex Record Office, 56, 104

Jack Wetter, front cover

Richard Williamson, 86, 88-96

About the Authors

IAN McINTYRE began sailing in Chichester Harbour in an 18-foot wooden dayboat some thirty years ago. He now owns a Sadler 34, and with his wife and friends enjoys exploring the English Channel coast from his base at Emsworth where he is an active member of the Sailing Club; he is also a committee member of the Friends of Chichester Harbour. Ian started his career in journalism, then switched to public relations, becoming Head of PR at ICI and then later at the World Wide Fund for Nature. Before his recent retirement he ran his own consultancy, specialising in environmental and marine issues.

JULIAN MARSHALL, a keen local sailor, is both an artist and writer. Chiefly a printmaker, she paints, has a special love for charcoal drawing and illustrates articles and books. She exhibits widely and in 2002 was Artist in Residence at Europos Parkas in Lithuania. Julian has written a number of travelogues and historical articles and enjoys travel, especially to less visited places like Greenland, Spitzbergen and the Ukraine in search of material for her sketchbooks and exhibitions.

MONIKA SMITH was born and educated in Germany. She came to London in 1970 where she worked as an interpreter and research librarian for a film, TV and theatrical costumier. She went on to study art and photography and then studied at the University of Sussex. Since the 1980s Monika has specialised as a freelance photo-journalist, working for a museum, a picture library and a print and publicity company. She writes regularly for local newspapers and a monthly feature on towns and villages in *Sussex Life*.

RUTH TITTENSOR is an ecologist, a chartered biologist, landscape historian, and Associate of the AHRB Centre for Environmental History, University of St Andrews. She first walked and worked in Chichester Harbour in 1972 when mapping the intertidal zone from end to end. Since then Ruth has carried out many ecological studies of the wide variety of habitats which make up the farmland, woods and coastline of the harbour, and has carried out extensive research into the history of landscapes in West Sussex.

RICHARD WILLIAMSON is the son of novelist and natural history writer Henry Williamson of *Tarka the Otter* fame. After the RAF and the forestry service he joined the Nature Conservancy, managing Kingley Vale National Nature Reserve for thirty-two years. Now retired, he still continues his researches into its birds, plants and butterflies. Richard wrote the first conservation plan for Chichester Harbour and has been involved in waterfowl counts there for forty years. With three books published, there are more in the pipeline, including his new novel set in both Chichester Harbour and Russia - *With Love from Russia* - about a Brent Goose and a lonely Russian girl.

INDEX

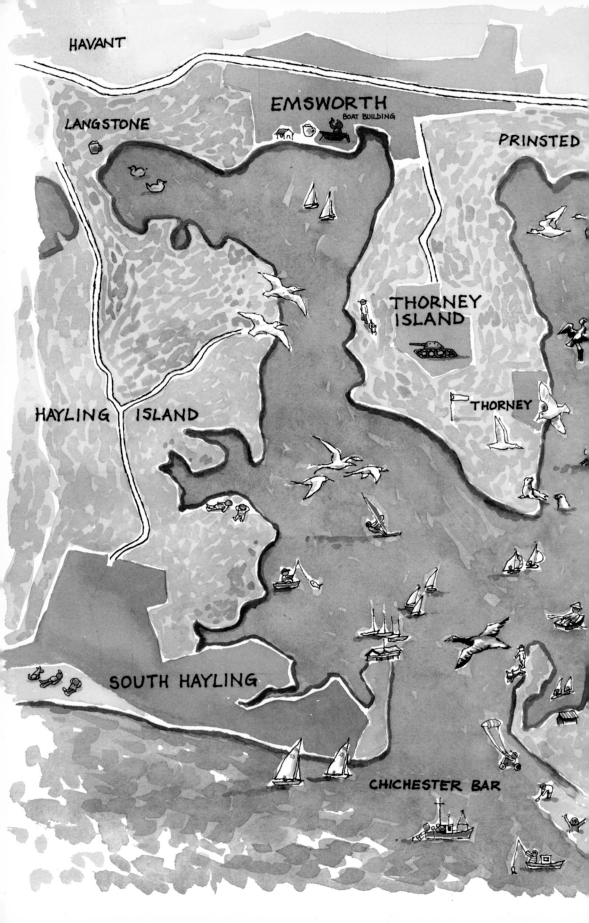